The Position
of Women in Islam

The Position
of Women in Islam

A Progressive View

Mohammad Ali Syed

State University of New York Press

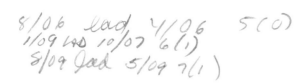

Published by
State University of New York Press, Albany

For information, address the State University of New York Press,
90 State Street, Suite 700, Albany, NY 12207

Production by Michael Haggett
Marketing by Anne M. Valentine

Library of Congress Cataloging-in-Publication Data

Ali, Syed Mohammed.
    The position of women in Islam : a progressive view / Mohammad Ali Syed.
      p. cm.
    Includes bibliographical references and index.
    ISBN 0-7914-6095-9 (alk. paper) — ISBN 0-7914-6096-7 (pbk. : alk. paper)
    1. Women in Islam.   2. Women in the Hadith.   3. Women's rights—
Religious aspects—Islam.   I. Title.

BP173.4.A45 2004
297'.082—dc22   2004045441

                      10 9 8 7 6 5 4 3 2 1

Contents

Preface

The early 1930s were a period of great change in the social, cultural, and political life of India. As a child born at that time, I was thrown into a melting pot that contained old conservative ideas and notions along with new ideas and aspirations that cried out for a change. In my early childhood, however, I was not aware of this situation. Born into a highly politicized and intellectual middleclass Muslim family of Calcutta, India, I was not only unaware of the restless nature of my society but perhaps I was misled by the liberal and progressive atmosphere in my family, which I assumed to be reality. To me, the rights, duties, and status of men and women in my society were not different. Exposed to the world outside my family in my teenage years, I was surprised to find how wrong I was. It was shocking to discover that women and particularly Muslim women in Bengal enjoyed hardly any status unless the elevated status of the domestic servant in a Bengali family could be considered any status at all. Why then was I so ignorant of the reality prevailing in the Muslim society of Bengal? The answer to this question was not far to seek. My father and all adult male members of my family were not only good Muslims but were very knowledgeable about Islam. The background of their tolerance and egalitarian attitude towards women was behind my illusion. I call it an illusion because the situation outside my family was completely different from that which I had observed in my family. In fact, our family was a very small island in the vast ocean of reactionary and antiwomen Muslim society of Bengal back then. I was disturbed and bewildered. I was doubly shocked when informed by the figures of authority in Bengali Muslim society that the inequality between men and women, which relegated women to a role inferior to men, was sanctioned by Islam. I did not like the assessment of the status of Muslim women suggested by these men of authority on Islamic law. Like the Turkish poet Zia, I asked myself, "How could the holy law of God regard these beautiful creatures (my mother, my sister, my daughter) as despicable beings? Surely, there is an error in the representation of the Quran by the learned."

The answer to my question was not readily available, but I was determined to find out the correct answer to this difficult question. I told myself, if there was an error in the representation of Islam by the framers of Islamic law (Shariah), then I must look at the original sources of these representations, for example the Quran (the revealed words of God) and the authentic Hadith (the sayings and deeds of the Prophet Muhammad (pbuh)) as supplemented by the various schools of Islamic law. To my joy and surprise I found the first two sources of Islamic law (the Quran and the Hadith) gave more rights to women than those recognized by the framers of Islamic law, who either misrepresented or partially represented the rights of Muslim women. However, although very pleasing to me, I realized that this newly acquired knowledge would be of very little use unless it was shared by Muslim society at large. This realization urged me to speak and write about the true messages of the Quran and those of the Prophet Muhammad (pbuh) concerning Muslim women to a wider audience. In seminars, lectures, and articles in England, the United States, Bangladesh, and India, I articulated my strongly fortified ideas about the elevated status of Muslim women. In 1998, in a seminar organized by The Muslims, an organization devoted to research on Islamic subjects, I presented a paper, "The Position of Women in Islam". My paper found a very sympathetic audience and I was encouraged to write a book on this subject.

I took this task in great seriousness and started searching for information from various authorities on the subject. Numerous English, French, German, American, Indian, Pakistani, South Asian, and Arab scholars helped me tremendously in my research. This in turn presented another problem, of sifting and funneling only the very essential information necessary for my book, to keep the book within a reasonable size. I considered the writings of the so-called champions of Islam who tried to portray Muslim women as having a very exalted position backed by only nice quotations from prominent authors without addressing the real issues, (i.e. the degraded position of Muslim women in modern society). I also looked into the remarks and opinions of conservative Muslim scholars who glorified the degraded status of modern Muslim women as being beneficial and befitting these women. I rejected the first group as more or less useless. As for the second group, I rejected them not only because they failed to supply sufficient authority from the Quran and the Hadith to justify their claim, but also because of their total lack of awareness of the serious problems faced by Muslim women in modern Muslim society needing urgent solutions. On the other end of the spectrum, there were vast materials supplied by the critics of Islam depicting the degraded status of Muslim women. These critics of Islamic values unreasonably blamed Islamic law for this phenomenon without supplying sufficient authority from the Quran or the authentic Hadith to sustain their claims. These authors were of very little help as they failed to address the issue of the position of Muslim women as sanctioned by Islam, mainly by the Quran and the Hadith. It appeared to me very little comprehensive discussion about Muslim women's rights in the various spheres of their lives had ever been made, not to speak of the correlation of these rights with the authorities of the Quran and the Hadith.

This is where I have stepped in by writing this book. I have chosen subjects that are relevant for modern Muslim women in their everyday lives, particularly those subjects that are most controversial, and I have endeavored to present the views of the Quran and the Hadith on these subjects. For the sake of brevity, I have dealt less with the current position of Muslim women and more with the real position they are given by the Quran and the Hadith. I have done this in the hope that the legitimate rights conferred on women by Islam will automatically cancel out the current deprivations they suffer, which are contrary to Islam. In discussing these subjects, I start with the relevant verses of the Quran followed by the appropriate, authentic Hadith and have supplemented where necessary with relevant remarks and comments of Islamic authorities and scholars. I always emphasize the superior claim of the Quran over the Hadith, and that of the Hadith, over the opinions of the various schools of Islamic law and other Islamic authorities. In fact, these sources and authorities comprise the majority of my work, the remaining portion being my own comments in areas where there is no compelling authority to follow and yet where an urgent answer is needed.

I am happy to mention the help that I have received from those very few pioneers of Islamic research who have served as models for my presentation. But I need to say they are the rare oases in the vast desert of ignorance and dogmatism. Finally, I cannot but admit that my conclusions may not always be flawless. However, I have attempted to present my views with the objectivity required for this serious subject, neither exaggerating Muslim women's rights as has been done by their champions nor minimizing them as conservative Muslim society has done. This book, I hope, will significantly fill the vast gap of knowledge in the study of the actual theoretical position of Muslim women as sanctioned by the Quran and the authentic Hadith.

Authors Note

As the author of this book, I owe explanations of certain matters that may raise controversies among the readers. On almost every topic dealt with in this book, I have questioned the traditional views of conservative Muslim scholars. In response to their possible criticism of my work, I can only point out that I have tried to state what the Quran and the authentic Hadith say and have highlighted where prevalent Islamic law has deviated from these two fundamental sources of Islamic law. To attain this objective, I quote Quranic verses and authentic Hadith supplemented by progressive authors who support my views. However, I have not failed to mention the views of those who contradict my views. The conclusions I arrive at are based more on these sources than on my own opinion. The authenticity of these conclusions is likely to be questioned by some traditional Islamic scholars. These same scholars may question my many references to works translated into English. For this I make no apology. However, I can mention my reasons for using these references. First, these authors are eminent scholars in their respective fields, and second, they have supported their opinions by English translations of the Quranic verses and authentic Hadiths. One such author is the translator of the Quran, Muhammad Ali, who belongs to the Lahori branch of the Ahmadi sect and believed Muhammad (pbuh) is the last Prophet. While considering the feelings of mainstream Muslims about the Ahmadis in general, I cannot ignore the valuable work of this outstanding scholar of Islamic law and issues. The great translator of the Quran into English, Abdullah Yusuf Ali, refers to Muhammad Ali on occasion. Another great translator of the Quran into English, Muhammad Marmaduke Pickthall, remarks, "Probably no living man has done longer or more valuable service for the cause of Islamic revival than Maulana Muhammad Ali of Lahore."

In order to allow the reader to examine some contoversial areas, I present some transliterations of Arabic Quranic verses in English. I present these especially in verses where different translators have translated them differently. Biblical English expressions such as thee, thou, hath, et cetera, used by Abdullah Yusuf Ali in his translation of the Quran have been substituted with modern English expressions, wherever necessary, for the convenience of the reader.

Another matter that constantly worried me was to avoid the reification of Islam in my work. I have tried to avoid it as much as possible. However, I was compelled to refer to the remarks of some authorities, who themselves indulged in reifying Islam. In such cases I paraphrased their remarks without making any fundamental alterations to these reified expressions. On my part, while avoiding expressions such as 'what Islam says,' I had no alternative but to use expressions such as 'Islamic law' or 'Islamic rules' in the same way as Christian scholars use expressions such as 'Canon law,' and 'Christian ethics.' However, when I have used the expressions 'the Quran teaches,' or 'the Hadith says,' I was not deliberately reifying Islam but actually referring to the two most important sources of Islamic law, namely the Quran and the Hadith. This could not be avoided.

In my work I have used abbreviations on very few occasions. The expression, pbuh, has been used after the Prophet, or Prophet Muhammad. The expression, pbuh, means peace be upon him. This expression signifies respect and is widely used in the Muslim world. My use of the expression, the Prophet (pbuh), is a substitute for the expression, the Prophet Muhammad (pbuh). With regards to Hadiths quoted in this book, the following abbreviations are used to indicate the collection of Hadiths from which it was taken:

AD   Abu-Daud
B   Bukhari
M   Muslim
N   Nesai
T   Tirmidhi

The author date system has been used for referencing. When AH is used, this indicates after Hijra, and indicates the cited reference was published using this dating system. For complete bibliographical details, see references.

Acknowledgments

It is difficult to convey my enormous gratitude to all those who have ungrudgingly helped me in the difficult endeavor of writing this book simply because the very list would tax the reader's patience. But even then, I cannot but express my deep appreciation to those whose help was exceptional. First and foremost I must express my deepest appreciation to my sons, Badrudduja Syed & Shamsuzzoha Syed, my daughter-in-law, Rawnaque Elahi-Syed, and my nephew, Arifur Rahman Khan, for their dedicated cooperation and help. This is no token acknowledgment. But for their untiring efforts and labor in helping to type the manuscript, it would not have been possible for this book to be published. To my son Shamsuzzoha, also goes the credit of constant counseling and painstaking care in revising and correcting the manuscript and for contacting various publishers on my behalf. To my daughter-in-law, Rawnaque Elahi-Syed, goes the credit of researching the marketing of this work. I am especially grateful to my friend and relative, Nurun Nabi Chowdhury (ex-Ambassador of Bangladesh to Egypt) who read most of the manuscript and made valuable comments.

I am under deep obligation to the pioneers of modern research on Muslim women, particularly Asghar Ali Engineer, Fatima Mernisi, and Amina Wadud Muhsin whose writings and works have had a profound influence in formulating my ideas and views. I use information and views from their works, and I can only hope this book will be a worthy continuation of their valued contributions in this field, particularly *The Rights of Women in Islam, Women and Islam,* and *The Quran and Women.* For translations of the Quran, I have depended mainly on the English translations of Abdullah Yusuf Ali and on occasions I have referred to the English translations of the Quran by Muhammad Ali. The English translations of the Quran by Muhammad Asad, Sayyid Qutb, Abul Kalam Azad, Mir Ahmed Ali, and others are mentioned in paraphrase only. In such cases I have indicated the translators name after such translation of the Quran.

I have carried out transliteration of Quranic verses myself, using the method of Muhammad Marmaduke Pickthall, another translator of the Quran.

I am very grateful to State University of New York Press for publishing this work. In particular, Nancy Ellegate, deserves my special acknowledgment. She was instrumental in supporting this work throughout the process of seeking approval for publication.

I shall fail in my duty if I do not record my unlimited appreciation and thanks to my loving wife, Momtaz Begum Syed. If it was not for her persistent and forceful (at times unnerving and alarming) persuasion and inspiring encouragement, this book could never have been completed. I also take this opportunity to thank the countless admirers of my speeches and writings on this subject who constantly encouraged me to write this book. Finally, my gratitude goes to Almighty God due to whose unlimited mercy this book has ultimately seen the light of day.

Introduction

The question of women's rights and obligations, in my opinion appear to be the most controversial and most complex of all social problems. According to Carol Tarvis and Carol Wade (1984), it has always been assumed throughout the centuries by all societies that the difference between males and females is not confined to basic anatomy but in their respective abilities to think and act. A historical study of the existence of differences between men and women in various societies leads to the conclusion that these differences are indications of different values as well. Because of the values and culture of male domination and of discrimination against women, the position of women in the western world was no better then their position in Asia and Africa. What is worse is that women were unaware of their rights even in the west until the beginning of the nineteenth century AD when western women fought for the recognition of their rights denied for centuries and the struggle for their rights came into focus with the suffragette movement in the beginning of the twentieth century. This gave birth to women's liberation movements in various parts of Europe and the Americas. Starting with the Married Women's Property Act 1882 and ending for the time being with the Pension Act 1995, women in the United Kingdom have slowly gained their economic, social, and political freedom denied to them earlier. Unfortunately, the attitude of the Christian church, until the end of the eighteenth century A.D., was not very friendly towards women and this caused further difficulties. However, the process of reinterpreting Christian texts and the restating of its values in the nineteenth and the twentieth centuries have been of immense help to Christian women.

In pre-Islamic Arabia the position of women was even worse. Women were treated as nothing but chattel. Married women were treated as heritable property, to be inherited by the heirs of a husband. In this dark era for women, Islamic reforms through the Quran and the Hadith of the Prophet Muhammad (pbuh) were revolutionary. Due to these Islamic

1

reforms, between 610 and 632 A.D. Muslim women gained rights unparalleled in the world. In fact, Muslim women enjoyed more rights than women in any other society until the liberation of women in the western world. The Quran, the principal authority for all Islamic rules and regulations, put women on an almost equal footing with their male counterparts, and the rights conferred on Muslim women by the Quran were supported and supplemented by the authentic Hadith of the Prophet Muhammad (pbuh).

However, from the very beginning of the Islamic era (610 A.D. onwards) male-dominated Arab society resisted the ideals of sexual equality prescribed by the Quran and the Hadith. By the time Islamic law (Shariah) began to be codified in the eighth century A.D. all sorts of pre-Islamic (Arab) and non-Islamic influences (from the Hellenic and Sassanid culture) had affected the thinking of the Muslim jurist. Conservatives and the traditionalists upheld the status quo of male domination of pre-Islamic Arab society and endeavored to justify their position. Explaining the situation in her book, *Women in the Quran*, Barbara Fryer Stowasser (1994) concludes that to attain the goal of preserving the stable structure of the past tradition of Muslim society prescribing inferior position to women compared to that of men, the conservative Muslim jurists justified through *ijma* (community consensus) of the conservative interpretation of the Quran and of the Hadith. This was, according to Stowasser, a defensive measure of the conservatives against anything western or modern. The feminist response to the conservative stand on women, although feeble, began to be noticed in the beginning of the twentieth century and more so in the eighties and the nineties of the twentieth century. The illegitimate imposition of inequality on Muslim women was challenged by prowomen groups of scholars and activists despite the hostile reception by conservative Muslim society. The two opposing groups of prowomen and antiwomen tendencies in Islamic theology and jurisprudence had their champions in Fatima Mernisi of Morocco, and Abbas Mahmud al-Aqqad of Egypt, respectively. Abbas Mahmud al-Aqqad (1959) espresses his total contempt for women of all societies by denying them any role other than raising children. According to al-Aqqad, women have never been a source of ethics or good conduct and men are the sole source of these things. Syed Qutb (1980), a greater scholar of Islamic law, refutes al-Aqqad's hostile opinion against women by asserting the distinction in their primordial nature has no inherent value so far as their capacity to act or think. Fatima Mernissi (1991) boldly challenges the antiwomen establishment in Muslim society by asserting the real reason behind the antagonism against Muslim women by the male elite is the conflict of their interests with those of women. Mernissi goes further by stating that the subjective view of these men about the culture and society of Muslims have no sacred sanction either from the Quran or the Prophet Muhammad (pbuh) or even from the early traditions of Muslim society. In Mernissi's book, one has a glimpse of the exalted position of honor and dignity enjoyed by Muslim women in the early days of Islam as the direct result of the mission of the Prophet Muhammad (pbuh). Of course, the Muslim woman's position is far from an exalted one today. This is surprising and unacceptable in light of the rights conferred on women by Islam over 1400 years ago. The main theme of this book is to challenge this current deprivation of Muslim women's legitimate rights by the conservative framers of Islamic law (Shariah).

Chapter 1 is an exploration of the respective roles of the Quran and the Hadith in Islamic law, emphasizing the Quran's role as the supreme authority. A discussion of these two primary sources of Islamic law is carried out in this chapter. Special emphasis is given to the fact that these sources supersede all claims by all authorities including the founders of the four schools of Sunni law. In Chapter 2, a discussion is held on the reward and punishment of men and women as prescribed by the Quran pointing out clearly that both the sexes are treated equally by God in the life hereafter. Chapter 3 looks at the Quran's dealing with the origin of men and women. In this chapter it is shown the Quran prescribes complete equality of men and women regarding their origin. Once the Quran's attitude towards women is clarified in these chapters, it is quite logical to turn to the totally contradictory ideas presented by some alleged sayings of the Prophet Muhammad (pbuh). This is carried out in chapter 4. This chapter questions the authenticity of these alleged sayings and shows why they cannot be accepted as genuine.

"Rules of Marriage in Islam" is the title of the chapter 5. Starting with various forms of marriage in pre-Islamic Arabia as the background of Islamic rules on this subject, a discussion is held of why *muta* (temporary) marriage, concubinage, and the rules of *akfa* are contrary to the rules of marriage in Islam. The chapter then turns to discuss specific aspects of Islamic marriage including: the independence of Muslim women to marry without a marriage guardian; child marriages; polygamous marriages; and marriages of Muslims with non-Muslims. The marriages of Muslims with non-Muslims is a particularly important and relevant issue in our global age. Chapter 6 explores the respective positions of the husband and wife as prescribed by Islam and whether equality exists within this relationship. Chapter 7's subject matter is rules of dissolution of marriage in Islam. This chapter is subdivided into three topics, namely, unilateral dissolution of the marriage by the husband; the wife's right to divorce her husband; and the roles of the court and of the arbitrators in the dissolution of marriage. When discussing the unilateral dissolution of the marriage by the husband, special attention is paid to the current practice of *talaq* (divorce) in one sitting and dispensing with the intervention of arbitrators in *talaq*. Chapter 8 addresses the rights of men and women in custody and access to children.

Chapter 9 deals with the financial and economic provisions for women in Islam. This chapter is divided into three subtopics, namely, women's rights of inheritance; women's rights of maintenance from her husband or from her husband's estate; and women's right of *mahr* (dower). The inferior rights of women in inheritance have traditionally been controversial. When addressing this issue in chapter 9, it is shown that the lesser rights of women can be remedied by the wills of a testator.

Islamic rules regarding women as witnesses, are discussed in chapter 10. An attempt is made in this chapter to remove any doubt about women's equality with men in this sphere, and the true Islamic provisions are pointed out.

Chapters 11 and 12 deal with two of the most controversial topics relating to women. In discussing Islamic rules regarding the seclusion of women in chapter 11, it is pointed out that current Islamic practice in many parts of the world is far from the rules laid down by the Quran and the Hadith. The questionable practice of seclusion of Muslim women in some societies is challenged, and a woman's right to participate in all activities of society is affirmed. Chapter 12 explores a woman's right to participate in politics and to become a head of state. This subject has invited a great deal of interest among both Muslims and non-Muslims, especially since the election of three Muslim women to the position of prime minister namely Benazir Bhutto in Pakistan, and Khaleda Zia and Hasina Wajed in Bangladesh. Refuting an alleged saying of the Prophet (pbuh) opposing women's promotion to the position of head of state, an endeavor is made to establish that there is nothing wrong or un-Islamic for a Muslim woman to be elevated to this position.

It is hoped this book will introduce the reader to the basis for calling for a radical reform of the position of Muslim women in the present day. Muslim women today deserve at least the same rights conferred to women of the Prophet's (pbuh) time. Perhaps the changes required to transform the theoretical rights into practical rights have only begun.

1

Roles of the Quran
and the Hadith in Islamic Law

The Quran (which is believed by Muslims to be the word of God) was revealed in stages during the twenty-two years of the prophethood (*risalat*) of the Prophet Muhammad (pbuh). During the same period, the Prophet (pbuh) made statements and gave his approval or disapproval on various religious, moral, social, cultural, and legal issues. These statements are called Hadiths and were collected by various Hadith collectors. Both the Quran and the Hadiths made it absolutely clear the Quran was the supreme and ultimate authority and a guide for all Muslims in all matters. The authority of the Hadith is next to that of the Quran. Thus the Quran states:

- "This is the Book; in it is guidance sure to those who fear God." (2:2)

- "... Say: 'It is not for me, of my own accord, to change it. I follow naught but what is revealed to me: if I were to disobey my Lord, I should myself fear the Penalty of a Great Day (to come).'" (10:15) (The expression 'say' refers to the Prophet (pbuh) and the expression 'change it' refers to the changing of the Quran.)

- "Your companion is neither astray nor being misled. Nor does he say (aught) of (his own) desire. It is no less than Inspiration sent down to him." (53:2–4) (The expression, Your companion, refers to the Prophet (pbuh) and the word, It, refers to the Quran.)

5

A famous saying of the Prophet Muhammad (pbuh) reported by Imam Shafii (1987) clarifies the situation further. Prophet Muhammad (pbuh) is reported to have said, "Compare what purports to come from me with the book of God. What agrees with it, I have said; what disagrees with it, I have not said."

However, problems arose when the Quran was silent on a particular point and Quranic provisions needed to be clarified or supplemented. In such circumstances, the aid of the Hadith (the saying, practices, approvals, and disapprovals of the Prophet Mohammad) were essential supplements to the Quran in formulating various Islamic rules. However, the use of the Hadith as the second source of Islamic law (Shariah) created problems that were completely unforeseen. Despite the Prophet's (pbuh) clear warning to Muslims to ignore any alleged Hadith which was in conflict with the Quran, many Islamic jurists and theologians overemphasized the Hadith to the extent of giving the Hadith precedence over the Quran. Another serious problem was posed by the introduction of a large number of forged Hadiths into the Muslim community by a motivated person or group. It is important to explore in detail how and why some Muslims gave the Hadith such importance as it has had a significant impact on the development of Islamic law.

Among the jurists and the theologians who overemphasized the importance of the Hadith, the first and foremost was Imam Shafii, the founder of the Shafii School of Sunni Law. Arguing on the basis of various Quranic verses, particularly 10:15 and 53:2–4, which, according to Shafii, equated the will of the Prophet (pbuh) with the will of Allah, Shafii opined that the extra-Quranic utterances of the Prophet (pbuh) (the Hadiths) were of divine origin like the Quran. According to Imam Shafii there are two types of revelations; the words of Allah (the Quran) and the words of the Prophet (pbuh) (the Hadiths). Shafii further argues that God appointed the Prophet (pbuh) to both deliver and interpret the minutest details of the revelations and that both functions (of the Prophet (pbuh)) are covered in the Quranic command for men to obey the Prophet (pbuh) in all things (Burton 1994). Shafii based this argument on a Hadith of the Prophet Mohammad (pbuh) in which he said: "I have omitted to command nothing that God commanded, and have omitted to prohibit nothing that God prohibited." However, Goldziher (1971) states that Imam Shafii did not believe a Hadith, even if well authenticated, could abrogate the Quran. In reality, the Prophet Muhammad (pbuh) had given clear instructions to discard any Hadith that disagreed with the Quran in the following words: "Compare what purports to come from me with the Book of God. What agrees with it, I have said; what disagrees with it, I have not said" (Shafii 1987). Yet, Imam Shafii preferred an alleged Hadith of the Prophet which said: "Let me not find any of you who says when a command and/or prohibition that I have uttered comes to him, 'I don't know, We shall follow what we find in the Book of God.'"

According to Shafii (1987), "The Hadith, vis-à-vis the Quran are of three categories:

1. Where there is a text in the Quran and the relevant Hadith of the Prophet (pbuh) conforms with the said Quranic text.

2. Where the text of the Quran is couched in general terms and the Hadith illustrated the precise meaning that was intended by the said text of the Quran.

3. When there is a Hadith on a topic on which the Quran is silent."

The Islamic jurists are in agreement with the first two categories. However, some Islamic scholars insist the Prophet (pbuh) never instituted any ruling on any matter unless it was referred to, at least in principle, in the Quran for example the obligation to pray in the Quran and the Prophet's (pbuh) Hadith giving details about the method of prayer (Burton 1994). Shah Waliullah Dahlavi (n.d.) mentions an authentic Hadith in which the Prophet Muhammad (pbuh) said, "The Quran can cancel the Sunnah of the Prophet (pbuh) but the Sunnah of the Prophet (pbuh) cannot cancel the Quran" (M 1:6–11).

In the generation that followed Imam Shafii, some Islamic jurists went to the opposite view by holding the opinion that if the Quran can abrogate the Hadith, the Hadith of the Prophet (pbuh) can abrogate the Quran, since Gabriel brought the Hadith from God, and one form of revelation can abrogate the other. In support of this opinion, they quoted an alleged Hadith of the Prophet (pbuh) in which he is alleged to have said, "I have been granted the Book and along with it's equal" (the Hadith) and 59:7 verse of the Quran which states: ". . . so take what the Apostle assigns to you, and deny yourselves that which he withholds from you. And fear God; for God is strict in punishment." It should be noted that this verse of the Quran deals with the Prophet's order or decision regarding shares of the booties of war for various groups of Muslims. Therefore, this verse cannot be used as an argument for giving the Hadith equal importance with the Quran. Ibne Kathir (1966) crystallizes this extreme opinion and says, "The Sunnah prevails over the Quran; the Quran does not prevail over the Sunnah." Arriving at this extreme position, these jurists ignored the principles on which Islam was founded and challenged the supreme authority of the Quran in Islamic law over everything including the Hadith. The fact that an alleged Hadith that contradicted the Quran could not have come from the Prophet Muhammad (pbuh) and therefore should be rejected was ignored. This had serious consequences for the development of Islamic law.

The serious problem of dealing with innumerable forged Hadiths demanded the attention of Muslim jurists and theologians in all ages. The first situation to consider in this area is a Hadith that contradicts another Hadith. Obviously, both cannot be authentic. The second situation arises when there are irreconcilable views of two collectors of Hadiths who are called traditionalists or *muhaddes*. The comments of Shibli Numani (1987) on this subject are worth noting. According to Numani, there are considerable differences among the traditionalists about the correctness or otherwise of a particular Hadith, one accepts it as a genuine (*sahih*) Hadith and the other rejects it as weak (*zaif*). Numani refers to Ibn Jauzi, a traditionalist who supports Numani's view about *zaif* Hadiths and even describes some Hadiths in the collections of Imam Bukhari and Imam Muslim as forgeries. The collections of Hadiths compiled by Imam Bukhari and Imam Muslim are considered by the Sunnis as the most reliable books after the Quran. However, Darqutuni, a collector of Hadiths from the fourth century AH wrote a special work showing the weakness of 200 Hadiths included in these two compilations (Goldziher 1971). It is interesting to note that Imam Bukhari criticizes Imam Muslim, and Imam Muslim criticizes Imam Bukhari even calling him a plagiarist and one who insults Hadiths (Mulki 1981). Imam Bukhari recognizes 434 reporters Imam Muslim does not cite, and Imam Muslim cites 625 reporters Imam Bukhari does not mention. It should also be noted Bukhari is stricter than Muslim regarding *isnad* (chain of authority) and insists that two men named consecutively in the *isnad* must have met. But Imam Muslim was content with evidence that two men named consecutively in the *isnad* were contemporaries and could have met (Burton 1994). All these complications regarding the authenticity of many Hadiths and their contradictions are the result of the introduction of many false and forged Hadiths. Alfred Guillaume (1954) gives a list of six alleged Hadiths that were contradicted by either the Quran, by another Hadith, or were contrary to reason. According to Guillaume, the Mutazilite (school of Islamic philosophy) are severe critics of the Hadiths.

Another critic of the Hadith, Goldziher (1971), gives reasons for the forged Hadiths. Goldziher suggests the deliberate inventions of these Hadiths were done either to justify existing local usage or to support the various views of divergent scholars working together in different legal schools of the Muslims. Inventions of these false Hadiths, according to Goldziker, were done with the purely selfish motive of securing support for the consensus of opinions (*ijma*) of the conservative Muslim jurists about their views on rituals, and legal, social, and political issues. Commenting on this extreme view of Goldziher, Burton (1994) states that Goldziher does not exempt any class of Hadiths from an allegation of falsehood.

Further difficulty was encountered in authenticating a Hadith when its narrator had either indulged in lying in their daily activities or when they were dealing in matters for which they were not qualified. Imam Malik (1981), the founder of the Maliki school of Sunni Law, laid down two tests for the acceptance of a narrator of Hadith in the following words, "I had the good fortune to be born in Medina at a time when 70 persons who were the *Ashabs* of the Prophet (pbuh) who could recite the Hadiths were still alive. They used to go to the mosque and would start speaking, 'the Prophet (pbuh) said so and so.' I did not collect any of the Hadiths that they recounted, not because these people were not trustworthy, but because I saw that they were dealing in matters for which they were not qualified. There were some people whom I rejected as narrators of Hadiths, not because they lied in their role as men of science by recounting false Hadiths that the Prophet (pbuh) did not say, but just simply because I saw them lying in their relations with people in their relationship that had noting to do with religion" (Al-Barr n.d.). Thus, according to Imam Malik, a narrator of Hadith could not be accepted if he was not well versed in Islamic law or found to be lying in any sphere of life. Sir Abdur Rahim (n.d.) in his *Principles of Muhammadan Jurisprudence* mentions *ashabs* of the Prophet (pbuh), who were traditionalists and jurists of Islamic law. They were Abu Bakr, Umar Bin Khattab, Ali Ibne Abutaleb, Ayesha Siddiqa, and Abu Musa al-Ashari. Among the *ashabs* who were traditionalists but not jurists of Islamic law were Abu Huraira and Anas Bin Malik. As the reporting of Hadiths suffered from the possibility of fallibility due to lapses of memory, many *ashabs*, being conscious of a possible lapse of memory, refused to report any Hadith for which they were otherwise qualified. One such companion of the Prophet (pbuh) was Umar Ibn Hasin, who made the following remark, "If I wanted to, I could recite traditions about the Prophet (pbuh) for two days without stopping. What kept me from doing it was that I had seen some of the companions of the messenger of Allah (pbuh) who heard exactly what I myself heard, who saw what I saw, and those men recounted Hadiths. Those traditions were not exactly what we heard. And I am afraid of hallucinating as they hallucinate."

Some Muslim scholars like Abu Zahra and Qadi Ayad give some support to the accusation of Goldziher against the Hadiths regarding the stigma of falsehood. Abu Zahra (n.d.) informs us that one of the reasons for the increase in lying concerning the Prophet (pbuh) and the schisms and divisions in the ranks of Islamic jurists, was the dissension tearing the Muslim world into civil war and schism leading to the birth of two Muslim sects, the Shiahs and the Sunnis (Zahra n.d.). According to Abu Zahra, the liars who tried to put words into the mouth of the Prophet (pbuh) to benefit their cause or party were innumerable. These liars are classified into three categories. The first category are those who attributed to the Prophet (pbuh) remarks he did not make and there are two groups in this category. The first group are those who lied for material advantages and the second group are those who lied for ideological advantages. The second category simply falsified the chain of authority (*isnad*) without fabricating the contents of the Hadith (*matn*) giving false *isnad* with famous persons to weak Hadiths. The third category are those who claim to have heard remarks they never heard or to have met people they never met.

Following the lead given by Goldziher, many western scholars challenged every Hadith until its authenticity was proved. Taking an extreme position against all Hadiths, Schacht (1950) commented that until authenticity was proven, every Hadith on legal issues must be considered nonauthentic, and a false expression of a legal opinion arrived at a date later than the time of the Prophet Muhammad (pbuh). Some western scholars such as Professor N. J. Coulson (1964), took a central position, suggesting the most reasonable principle of historical inquiry should be to accept an alleged Hadith as genuine unless there are reasonable bases or convincing arguments that indicate the fictitiousness of the said Hadith. We have already seen that long before the strict test of Goldziher, Muslim authorities on the Hadith accepted the fact that many false Hadiths were in circulation. They went even further by making elaborate rules of criticism to determine the authenticity of any Hadith. Shah Abdul Aziz Dahlavi (n.d.) has summarized the rules of criticism of Hadiths.

He states that a report of a Hadith will not be accepted under any of the following circumstances:

- If the report was against the plain teachings of Islam.

- If the report was against reason.

- If the report contained threats of heavy punishment for ordinary sins or of mighty reward for the slight good deeds.

- If the report spoke of rewards form the Prophets and messengers instead of from Allah for the doers of good deeds.

- If the subject matter or words of the report were '*rakik*' (unsound or incorrect) e.g. if the subject matter was unbecoming of the Prophet's (pbuh) dignity or the words of the report were not in accordance with the Arabic idioms.

- If the report was reported by a single man while it was of such a nature that to know it or to act upon it was incumbent upon all.

- If the report was opposed to recognized historical facts.

- If the report was reported by only one reporter and had the reported incident happened it would have been known and reported by a large number of reporters.

- If the narrator had confessed that he had fabricated the report.

- If the time and circumstances of the narration of the reporter contained evidence of its forgery.

- If the report was an uncorroborated report of a Shiah reporter accusing the Sahabas or if the report of a Khariji reporter accusing a member of the Prophet's (pbuh) family."

Similar rules of criticism of Hadiths were laid down by Mulla Qari in *Maudzat,* Ibnul Jauzi, in *Fathul Mugith,* and Ibne Hajar, in *Nuzhat An-Nazar.* Ibne Hajar (n.d.) states that among the reasons for rejecting an alleged Hadith as authentic is its subject matter. According to Hajar, if a Hadith contradicted the Quran, a recognized Hadith, the unanimous opinion of Muslim society, or common sense, it should be rejected. Summarizing the whole matter concerning the verification of the authenticity of any Hadith in the various collections of Hadiths, Muhammd Ali (1950) holds the view that despite the fact all the collections of authentic (*sahi*) Hadiths had been made by reputed experts on Hadiths (*muhaddesses*), it cannot be claimed that one-hundred percent of their judgements are correct and therefore other Muslims might have their own judgements. It is noteworthy that traditionalists including Imam Bukhari never claimed faultlessness in their collections of Hadiths. In fact, they left the question of the reliability of the Hadith in their collections of Hadith to the generations that followed them.

Questioning the good memory and trustworthiness of the reporters in the chain of authority (*isnad*) of reports, which contradicted the Quran or reason, Fatima Mernissi (1991) argues for a vigilant examination of all Hadiths including the so-called *sahih* (authentic) Hadiths of the *Siha Sittas* (the six collections of authentic Hadiths). According to Mernissi, Imam Malik bin Anas sanctions this right for every Muslim. Mernissi further argues that collectors of Hadiths, including Imam Bukhari, declare their fallibility, acknowledging that only God is infallible. Therefore, she claims that questioning everything and everybody, including the jurists of Islamic law and the collectors of Hadiths by the Muslims, is a right sanctioned by Islamic tradition. Furthermore, Mernissi urges Muslims to find out the true traditions that have been obscured by centuries of neglect.

When summarizing the respective roles of the Quran and the Hadith in formulating Islamic law, it is essential to remember that the Quran is the primary source of information and the Hadith is an important, but secondary, source of information. The promotion of the Hadith to an equal status with the Quran is not sanctioned by fundamental Islamic principles but has unfortunately been encouraged by misinformed or ill-motivated jurists of Islamic law. The added factor of false Hadiths has complicated the matter. It is imperative that the ability to reject alleged Hadiths that do not fulfill the criteria of authenticity described above be retained by Muslims formulating Islamic law in the present day. If this ability is not retained then Islamic law will be polluted by alleged sayings of the Prophet that have been forged in the centuries since his death. It would be highly unfortunate if this is allowed as it would result in Islamic laws that are not true to the original teachings of the Prophet Muhammad (pbuh).

2

Reward and Punishment of the Sexes by God as Prescribed by the Quran

The following verses of the Quran deal with reward and punishment by God. They clearly demonstrate the Quran's equal treatment of male and female in this sphere. They refer neither to male nor female but to people irrespective of their sex.

- "Who can be better in religion than one who submits his whole self to God, does good, and follows the way of Abraham, the true in faith?" (4:125)

- "To those who believe and do deeds of righteousness has God promised forgiveness and a great reward.

   Those who reject faith and deny Our signs will be Companions of Hell-fire." (5:10–11) (The expression, Our signs, refers to God's revelations.)

- "Those who believe (in the Quran), those who follow the Jewish (scriptures), and the Sabians and the Christians—and who believe in God and the Last Day, and work righteousness, on them shall be no fear, nor shall they grieve." (5:72)

- "For those who believe and do righteous deeds, for them are Gardens as hospitable homes, for their (good) deeds.

   As to those who are rebellious and wicked, their abode will be the Fire . . ." (32:19–20)

- "God created the heavens and the earth for just ends, and in order that each soul may find the recompense of what it has earned and none of them be wronged." (45:22)

- " . . . Verily the most honoured of you in the sight of God is (he who is) the most righteous of you . . ." (49:13)

Yusuf Ali wrongly puts the expression 'he who is' in parenthesis as part of his translation of the above verse. This expression is not in the original Arabic of 49:13 of the Quran. It is perhaps because of this that he has entered this in parenthesis.

There are other Quranic verses for example, 4:1 and 7:189, which although meant for both sexes, refer specifically to men. The exclusion of women from the wording of these verses caused great distress to Muslim women during the Prophet Muhammad's (pbuh) lifetime. The revelation of verse 35 of Sura Ahzab removed to a great extent the grievances of the Muslim women caused by the men only verses of the Quran. Verse 33:35 was just the beginning of a new trend in Quranic revelations and many succeeding verses of the Quran deal with both men and women using separate expressions for both the sexes. Tabari (1979), the great historian and *mufassir* gives the background of the revelation in 33:35 in the following words. "Hazrat Umme Salama, one of the wives of the Prophet (pbuh) asked the Prophet (pbuh) one day. 'Why are men mentioned in the Quran and why are we (the women) not?' In those days men and women expected a response from Allah on the question of their status in the newly emerging Islamic Umma (the Muslim Community) and therefore Hazrat Umme Salama awaited anxiously for an appropriate revelation in reply to her specific question to the Prophet (pbuh)."

From the study of the history of the life of the Prophet (pbuh), we learn that whenever confronted with a difficult question, the Prophet (pbuh) thought deeply about the same and prayed earnestly for God's guidance through His revelation dealing with that particular question. One such revelation of God that answered the Prophet's (pbuh) prayer was 33:35 of the Quran. This verse addresses the complaint of Hazrat Umme Salama. Tabari (1979) mentions the very words of Hazrat Umme Salama on the occasion of the first recitation of 33:35 by the Prophet (pbuh) in a public place (the mosque). According to Tabari, Hazrat Umme Salama said:

"I had asked the Prophet (pbuh), 'why the Quran did not speak about us as it did of men,' and what was my surprise one afternoon when I was combing my hair, to hear his (the Prophet's pbuh) voice from the mimber. I hastily did up my hair and ran to one of the apartments from where I could hear better. I pressed my ear to the wall and here is what the Prophet (pbuh) said! "O People! Allah has said in his Book' and then he recited the verse 35 of Sura Ahzab (33:35) in the following words:

'For Muslim men and women—

For believing men and women,

For devout men and women,

For true men and women,

For men and women who are patient and constant,

For men and women who humble themselves,

For men and women who give in charity,

For men and women who fast (and deny themselves),

For men and women who guard their chastity, and

For men and women who engage much in God's praise—

For them has God prepared forgiveness and great reward.' "

According to Muhammad Ali (1951), 33:35 puts women on the same spiritual level with men by repeating ten times the good qualities of both men and women separately and by declaring the same rights of reward from God for both the sexes.

Some other verses of the Quran quoted below also mention men and women separately:

- "If any do deeds of righteousness—be they male or female, and have faith, they will enter Heaven, and not the least injustice will be done to them." (4:124)

- "And their Lord has accepted of them, and answered them: 'Never will I suffer to be lost the work of any of you, be he male or female: You are members, one of another...'" (3:195)

- "He that works evil will not be requited but by the like thereof, and he that works righteous deeds, whether man or woman—and is a Believer—such will enter the Garden (of Bliss): therein will they have abundance without measure." (40:40)

- "O you who believe! Let not some men among you laugh at others: It may be that the (latter) are better than the (former): Nor let some women laugh at others: It may be that the (latter) are better than the (former): Nor defame nor be sarcastic to each other, nor call each other by (offensive) nicknames: Ill-seeming is a name connoting wickedness, (to be used of one) after he has believed: And those who do not desist are (indeed) doing wrong." (49:11)

- "O mankind! We created you from a single (pair) of a male and a female, and made you into nations and tribes, that you may know each other (not that you may despise each other). Verily the most honoured of you in the sight of God is (he who is) the most righteous of you. And God has full knowledge and is well acquainted (with all things)." (49:13)

It is unfortunate that in history women have often been targeted as the sex more likely to indulge in backbiting and gossiping. It is noticeable that 49:11 criticizes persons of both genders for mocking, defaming, and backbiting fellow human beings. Commentating on 49:11 and 49:13, Syed Qutb (1980) opines that these verses are inclusive of all the variations among humankind: gender, colors et cetera, as all will return to the single scale of *taqwa* (God consciousness). According to Maudoodi (1983), 49:13 is addressed to the whole of mankind irrespective of race, color, language, country, and nationality. The significant omission of gender in his list of prejudices may be attributed to the conservative attitude of Maudoodi towards women, or it is possible his list was not exhaustive. It is noteworthy Maudoodi quotes a Hadith from the collection of Ibne Maja in the same page of his aforesaid comment. This Hadith states: "Allah does not see your outward appearance and your passion, but He sees your heart and your deeds." Hearts and deeds being genderless, even Maudoodi cannot deny this Hadith applies to both males and females.

The expression in 49:13, "Verily, the most honoured of you in the sight of God is (he who is) the most righteous of you" excluding the word in parenthesis emphatically supports the equality of men and women in the eye of God. The distinguishing value from God's perspective is righteousness and whoever (he or she) has the most righteousness is the noblest to God.

Perhaps the strongest support for the equality of men and women in the Quran is found in 4:124. This verse clearly states men and women will be rewarded equally based on their deeds. Verse 3:195 further supports the concept of equality in judging the work of members of both sexes. Even the most conservative Islamic jurist is unable to question the clarity of these verses in their equal treatment of men and women.

3

Origin of Men and Women According to the Quran

Like the reward and punishment of men and women by God, the Quran prescribes complete equality for men and women regarding their origin. The biblical story of the creation of Eve from a rib of Adam may be allegorical or literal, but the Quran totally rejects such an idea and no Hadiths support this biblical story. The following Quranic verses show the Quran stresses the common origin of the human race and both sexes have originated from one living entity (Asad 1984).

- *"Ya ayhuan naas attaqu rabbakum aallaazi khalaqa kum min nafsay waahay daatayn waa khalaqa minha zawjahaa wa baassan minhuma rejalaan kaasiraan waan nisa, waattaqu allah aal laazi taasaaluna bihi waal aarhama inna allah kaana aalaikum raakiba."*

    "O mankind! Reverence your Guardian-Lord, who created you from a single person, created, of like-nature, his mate, and from them twain scattered (like seeds) countless men and women; Fear God, through Whom you demand your mutual (rights), and (reverence) the wombs (that bore you): for God ever watches over you." (4:1)

- *"Huaallazi khalaqakum min nafsin waahaydaataan wa jaala minha zawjaha lay yaaskuna ilaiha"*

    "It is He who created you from a single person (nafsin), and made his mate of like nature, in order that he might dwell with her (in love) . . . " (7:189)

17

- *"Wa Allahu jaalaa laakum min aanfusaykum azwajan . . ."*
  "And god has made for you mates (and companions) of your own nature (*aanfusaykum*) . . ." (16:72)

- *"Wa min aayatayhi aan khalaqa laakum min aanfusaykum azwajan lay taaskunu ilayha . . ."*
  "And among his Signs is this, that he created for you mates from among yourselves (*aanfusaykum*), that you may dwell in tranquility with them . . ." (30:21)

- *"Khaalaqakum min nafsin wahaydaatin summa jaala minha zawjaha . . ."*
  "He created you (all) from a single person (*nafsin*): then created, of like nature, his mate . . ." (39:6)

- *"Faatirus saamaawaati wal ardhay. Jaala laakum min aanfusaykum azwajan . . ."*
  "(He is) the Creator of the heavens and the earth: He has made for you pairs from among yourselves (*aanfusaykum*) . . ." (42:11)

A careful examination of these six Quranic verses reveal the Quran mentions the creation of both men and women, both of them being created from *nafs* or *aanfus* (plural of *nafs*). Quoting Abu Muslim, Imam Razi interpretes *"khalaqa minha zawjahaa"* in 4:1 as meaning, "He created its mate (sexual mates for both male and female) out of its own kind (*min jinsha*). Imam Razi suggests that the word *nafs* may have four meanings, namely, soul; self; person or living person; or will or good pleasure. In his translation of the Quran, Abdullah Yusuf Ali (1946) accepts this construction of Imam Razi. Discussing the various meanings of *nafs*, Muhammad Abduh (n.d.) rejects most of the said interpretations including 'human being' and prefers 'human kind'. Muhammad Asad (1984) agrees with Abduh that the term 'human kind' gives emphasis to the common origin and brotherhood of the human race. According to Asad the expression *minha* meaning 'out of it' refers clearly to the biological fact of the common origin (one living entity) of both sexes.

Giving literal and etymological interpretations of three Quranic terms, namely, *nafs* (plural *aanfus*), *min*, and *zawj*, Amina Wadud Muhsin (1992) comments *Nafs* is grammatically feminine and takes corresponding feminine adjective and verbal antecedents. However, conceptually *nafs* is neither masculine nor feminine. According to Muhsim, these words are never used in the Quran with reference to any created self other than 'human kind.' She further asserts God never intended to begin the creation of human kind with a male and the Quran never refers to the origin of the human race with Adam. *Min* has two uses in the Arabic language and while its meaning 'from' it may be used to imply either 'extraction of a thing from' or 'of the same nature as.' *Zawj* (plural *azwaj*) is used in the Quran to mean mate, spouse, or group. *Zawj* is grammatically masculine and takes corresponding masculine verbal antecedents. However conceptually it is neither masculine nor feminine. For example, in 55:52 it is used for plants and in 11:40 it is used for animals. *Zawj* is also used to indicate females (eg. 4:20 and 2:102) as well as males (eg. 2:230 and 58:1) in the Quran. Muhsim concludes that the Quran states only two clear things about the creation of human kind, namely, human kind is from *nafs* and its mate (*zawj*) was created from *nafs*.

Commenting on 16:72, Muhammad Ali (1951) opines that the Quran states in this verse that wives of all men are created from their *aanfus* (plural of *nafs* meaning self or soul). He also rejects the Genesis story of the creation of Eve from the ribs of Adam, which according to him, was never mentioned in the Quran.

From the above discussion, it is clear that according to the verses of the Quran, men and women have a common origin and neither is superior to the other. Equality of men and women is emphasized by the Quran in all matters relating to the creation of mankind.

4

Assessment of Some Alleged Sayings of the Prophet Muhammad (pbuh)

Some alleged sayings of the Prophet Muhammad (pbuh) have been used by antiwomen sections of Muslim society to curtail women's rights. The alleged sayings have been used to maintain a false justification of the superiority of men over women. Eight of these alleged sayings, which are highly prejudicial to women, are given below and are then discussed to show why they should be rejected and why they cannot be accepted as authentic sayings of the Prophet Muhammad (pbuh).

1. "I took a look at Paradise and I noted that majority of the people there were poor, I took a look at Hell, and noted that women were the majority." (Bukhari)

   "I have seen that the majority of the dwellers of Hell Fire were you (women)." (B 1:131)

2. Abdullah Ibne Umar narrated the following alleged saying of the Prophet (pbuh): "I do not leave after me any cause of trouble more fatal to man than woman." (Bukhari)

3. "A woman cannot enter paradise if her husband is not pleased with her." (Tabrizi 1973)

4. "Had Sajda (prostration) not been prohibited, I would have ordered women to perform Sajda to their husbands."

5. Abu Hurayra narrated the following alleged saying of the Prophet (pbuh): "Three things bring bad luck: house, women and horse." (Bukhari)

Abdullah Ibne Umar narrated the following alleged saying of the Prophet (pbuh): "Evil omen is in the women, the house, and the horse." (B 7:030)

6. Abu Hurayra reported but subsequently retracted the following alleged saying of the Prophet (pbuh): "He whom the dawn finds sullied (*janaban*) (referring to being sullied by the sexual act) may not fast."

7. "The dog, the ass and the women interrupt prayer if they pass in front of the believers, interposing themselves between them and qibla." (Bukhari)

8. "I have not seen anyone more deficient in intelligence and religion than you (women)." (B 1:301)

The alleged Hadith to the effect that "the majority of the dwellers of paradise were poor and the majority of the dwellers of Hell were women" needs careful scrutiny as this alleged Hadith asks us to believe something that is unlikely for the Prophet (pbuh) to have said in view of his extreme regard and sympathy for women demonstrated by other authentic Hadith and by the history of his life. This alleged Hadith is definitely against one of the tests for an authentic Hadith, that is, it is unreasonable. One may ask how the Prophet (pbuh) could ever see all the inmates of heaven and hell and whether it was logistically possible for him to count these inmates to ascertain the majority and minority according to their sex and wealth. This alleged Hadith is also against the fundamental principle of equality of the sexes stated in the Quran and described in chapters 2 and 3 of this book. This alleged Hadith clearly fails the test of authenticating a Hadith as laid down by the Prophet (pbuh) when he said, "Compare what purports to come from me with the Book of God. What agrees with it, I have said; What disagrees with it, I have not said" (Shafii n.d.). In view of the above, it should be stated that despite allegedly being narrated by Ibne Umar and despite being part of the Sahih Bukhari, this alleged saying of the Prophet (pbuh) must be rejected as an authentic Hadith. Even Imam Bukhari did not claim infallibility and kept this alleged Hadith in his collection only on the basis of *isnad* (chain of authority). The Quran being infallible, this alleged statement cannot be accepted as an authentic Hadith as it contradicts the spirit and thrust of the Quran.

The alleged Hadith, "I do not leave after me any cause of trouble more fatal to man than woman" is so outrageous and so discriminatory it does not need much study and research to reject it. It fails all the tests of an authentic Hadith mentioned in chapter 1. It also contradicts the Quranic verses mentioned in chapter 2 of this book. Besides, the memory and trustworthiness of those in its *isnad* (the chain of authority) of this alleged Hadith are questionable. Therefore, it is safe to reject this Hadith. Finally, this alleged saying of the Prophet (pbuh) clearly contradicts Quranic verses 7:189 and 30:21 both of which mention the comfort and quiet of mind which husbands find from their wives.

The alleged saying of the Prophet (pbuh), "A woman cannot enter paradise if her husband is not pleased with her" cannot be accepted as an authentic Hadith because it not only violates all the tests of authenticating a Hadith but also contradicts the conclusions drawn in chapter 2 of this book on the reward and punishment of the sexes by God. Nowhere in that discussion is the said qualification required for a woman to enter paradise. There is one additional problem that arises for women who have more than one husband in succession. The question arises, which particular husband's pleasure is required for the woman to enter paradise? Finally, men and women can enter paradise only at God's pleasure and not at the pleasure of a human being, whatever his/her position.

The fourth alleged Hadith that states, "Had Sajda (prostration) not been prohibited, I would have ordered women to perform Sajda to their husbands," is one of the best examples of a questionable Hadith. There is no need for a Muslim to take this Hadith as the recommendation of the Prophet (pbuh) or as his order. It is impossible for the Prophet (pbuh) to have made such a remark, as the Prophet (pbuh), under no circumstance, would worship anybody other than Allah. This alleged Hadith is also against reason, as it does not include any proviso for the treatment of an undeserving husband by the wife. Therefore we can safely reject this Hadith as forged.

The alleged Hadith, "three things bring bad luck: house, women and horse" or "the evil omen is in the women, the house and the horse" need very careful examination. While including this alleged Hadith in his Sahih collection, Imam Bukhari fails to mention any refutation or contradictory version of this Hadith. The accepted rule is to give one or more contradictory version of any reported Hadith in order to present readers with conflicting points of view so they are sufficiently well informed to decide for themselves about the real position of the subject matter in any reported Hadith.

After thorough research of the Sahih Bukhari collection, Fatima Mernisi (1991) concludes there was no mention in that collection of Hazrat Aisha's refutation of this alleged Hadith (reported by Abu Hurayra)

regarding women bringing bad luck or being evil omens. Imam Zarakshi
(1980) mentions Ayesha's refutation of this particular Hadith. According
to Zarakshi, Aisha criticised Abu Hurayra for learning his lessons very
badly and for reporting only the second part of the Prophet's (pbuh)
remark on this matter. Ayesha comments that what the Prophet (pbuh)
had actually said was, "May Allah refute the Jews, they say three things
bring bad luck: house, women and horse." Ayesha also challenged many
other alleged Hadiths reported by Abu Hurayra. In his Sahih Hadiths,
Imam Bukari (1973), mentions Abu Hurayra's explanation for the im-
provement of his memory. According to Bukhari, Abu Hurayra mentioned his forgetfulness to the Prophet (pbuh) who miraculously improved
Abu Hurayra's memory by spreading his cloak while Abu Hurayra was
speaking to the Prophet (pbuh). Yet from studying the Prophet's (pbuh)
biography and history we find that despite the pressures of his companions the Prophet (pbuh) strongly opposed the idea of miraculous and
magical acts. In light of this, it is highly unlikely the Prophet (pbuh)
would give such miraculous help to Abu Hurayra. Regarding the report
of an alleged Hadith by Abdullah Ibne Umar, making the same comment
about women, Ayesha's refutation of the aforesaid report by Abu Hurayra
is enough justification to reject the said alleged Hadith.

Imam Zarakshi (1980) informs us about another false Hadith reported by Abu Hurayra. According to Zarakshi, Abu Hurayra reported
the Prophet (pbuh) had said, "He whom the dawn finds sullied by the
sexual act (janaban) may not fast." Zarakshi further comments that, being
confronted by other sahabas, after Hazrat Aisha and Hazrat Umme Salama
state the Prophet (pbuh) used to fast in the morning without making
ritual purification after spending the night janaban, Abu Hurayra confessed he had not heard the said Hadith himself. Just before his death,
Abu Hurayra completely withdrew his report about this alleged Hadith.

Alleged Hadith number 7 cited above states, "The dog, the ass and
women interrupt prayer if they pass in front of the believers, interposing
themselves between them and qibla." Imam Bukhari (1973) in the Sahih
Bukhari mentions Ibne Marzuq quoting Ayesha's comment on this alleged Hadith. Ibne Marzuk said that, having heard about the contents of
this alleged Hadith, Aisha expressed her sorrow that women are compared to dogs and asses. Marzuk further states that Ayesha said the Prophet
(pbuh) used to perform his prayers while she was there, lying on the bed
between him and the qibla. This alleged Hadith cannot be accepted as
authentic not only because of what Ayesha said about it, but also because
it is against reason. Prayer can be disturbed by various other interpositions

between one who prays and the *qibla*, and women cannot be bracketed with dogs and asses as interrupters of prayer. Besides, this alleged Hadith fails to inform us about the interrupters of women's prayer and whether men, passing in front of women believers, would break their prayers.

The alleged Hadith number 8, cited above, states women are more deficient in intelligence and religion. This cannot be accepted as an authentic Hadith of the Prophet (pbuh) as it fails the test of an authentic Hadith. It is unreasonable, not in conformity with the facts of history, and not in agreement with the Quran. Those who claim the authenticity of this Hadith argue on the basis of verse 4:5 of the Quran which states: "To those weak of understanding (*sufahaa*) do not make over your property, which God has made a means of support for you." However, without any basis for the inclusion of women and children among the *sufahaas*, they justify the exclusion of both these groups from inheritance on the basis of 4:5. The great interpreter of the Quran, Tabari (1984), challenged this illogical interpretation and extension of the term *sufahaa*. Commenting on this portion of 4:5, Tabari says, "According to us, the correct way of interpreting Allah's words,'Don't give to the foolish what is in your keeping of their wealth' is that God has used the word *sufahaa* in its general meaning and that he did not limit it to one precise category of foolish people." Therefore, according to Tabari, irrespective of the age or sex of the beneficiaries, this verse prohibits the handing over of a fortune to a foolish person who is incapable of managing properties that must be under the guardians of property. From this interpretation of 4:5, it is clear the verse relates only to the management of the property of foolish people and the expression 'foolish' is applicable to men and women irrespective of their age. This alleged Hadith also conflicts with the principle enunciated by a famous Hadith narrated by Caliph Ali and reported by Ibn Asakir. This Hadith says: "One who honours women is himself honoured and one who insults them is himself lowly" (Engineer 1992). This alleged Hadith also contradicts the principle of verse 71 of Sura Tauba of the Quran which states: "The Believers, men and women, are protectors, one of another: they enjoin what is just, and forbid what is evil" (9:71). The history of the Muslims is full of material about Muslim women taking leading roles in religious and intellectual fields. Thus, we find that Hazrat Khadija was the first believer of the Prophet's (pbuh) mission and Hazrat Hafsa was the custodian of the first compilation of the Quran made by the order of the Caliph Abu Bakr. Hazrat Ayesha distinguished herself as the great exigist of the Quran and a large part of her work in this field is included in the collection of Hadiths collected by Iman Muslim. Ayesha was also a great narrator of Hadiths. The Prophet (pbuh) had given tribute to her in saying that, "Half the knowledge of my revelation should be acquired from all of my companions and the other half from Aisha." Almost all the wives of the Prophet (pbuh) had expertise in the field of Hadith. Other women experts in Hadith who narrated a number of Hadith include Umme Hani, Asma Binte Abu Bakr, Umme Atiyaa, and Fatima Binte Qays. Among the women *ashabs* of the Prophet (pbuh), Rafidah Aslamiya, Umme Muta, Umme Kabsh, and several others were experts in medicine and in surgery. Rafidah Aslamiya had a nursing home next to the Prophet's (pbuh) mosque. In view of the above, it is clear this alleged Hadith should be condemned as a forgery.

From the above discussion it is also clear that the alleged sayings of the Prophet Muhammad (pbuh), which are discussed here, cannot be thought of as coming from him. In fact, it is an insult to the Prophet (pbuh) and his teachings to attribute such prejudicial and anti-women statements to his name. Neither the Quran nor authentic Hadiths allows such beliefs regarding women.

5

Rules of Marriage in Islamic Law

The only permissable sexual relationship under Islamic law is through marriage. Both the Quran and the Hadith prefer marriage to celibacy. The following Quranic verses show the Quran's attitude towards marriage:

- "It is He who has created man from water: then He has established relationships of lineage and marriage: for your Lord has power (over all things)." (25:54)

- "It is He who created you from a single person, and made his mate of like nature, in order that he might dwell with her (in love) . . . "(7:189)

- "And among His signs is this, that He created for you mates from among yourselves, that you may dwell in tranquility with them, and He has put love and mercy between your (hearts) . . . " (30:21)

- "(He is) the Creator of the heavens and the earth: He has made for you pairs from among yourselves, and pairs among cattle: by this means does He multiply you . . . "(42:11)

- "Marry those among you who are single, or the virtuous ones among your slaves, male or female: If they are in poverty, God will give them means out of His Grace . . . " (24:32)

- "Let those who find not the wherewithall for marriage keep themselves chaste, until God gives them means out of His Grace . . . " (24:33)

• "If any of you have not the means wherewith to wed free believing women, they may wed believing girls from among those whom your right hand possess: And God has full knowledge about your faith. You are one from another . . . " (4:25)

It is clear from the above Quranic verses that God prefers human beings to be married and when there is difficulty in finding a suitable match among believing women for any reason including poverty, then men are asked to marry their female slaves. Masters of the slaves, both male and female, are asked by the Quran to arrange for their marriage. The same support for marriage is found in the Hadith of the Prophet Muhammad (pbuh) when he said, "I fear Allah more than anyone else: I pray and fast and yet I marry women. And those who deviate from my practice are not from me" (Bukhari 1973). Regarding the nature of marriage, Quranic verse 4:21 calls it *mithaq*, or a solemn covenant. From this designation of marriage, most Islamic jurists agree that marriage is a contract under Islamic law. Since a contract cannot be made without the free consent of the two parties, under Islamic law, a marriage is a contract between two equal parties, that is, a man and a woman, neither of whom have special privileges over the other. Like any other contract, the parties to an Islamic marriage have every right to place special conditions as long as they do not violate the limits set by God. The essential elements of the contract of Islamic marriage are the *ijab* (affirmation or declaration of the proposal) and the *qubul* (acceptance of the proposal). Usually the proposal is made by the would-be husband and the acceptance of the proposal is made by the would-be wife. Like every contract, Islamic marriage must have a consideration, and according to the Quran (4:4) this is *saduqa*, or dower, which is a free gift to the wife from the husband. Verse 4:24 of the Quran, which says, " . . . seeing that you derive benefit from them (wives) give them their dowers as prescribed . . . " makes clear that the dower is a consideration of the marriage contract. Dower is prescribed even for female slaves married to a man according to verse 4:25. The other essential of the Islamic marriage is publicity of the marriage, which is ensured by witnesses. The Quran insists on the publicity of the marriage as the Quran prohibits secret sexual relationships. Hadiths also insist on such publicity and there are Hadiths, which say marriage must be made known publicly, even with the beating of drums. Verse 4:6 of the Quran says, "Make trial of orphans until they reach the age of marriage . . . " From this verse it can be deduced that the contract of marriage can be entered by only when a man or a woman has attained majority or marriageable age. According to Fyzee (1964) majority is attained at puberty and the presumption for the age of puberty is fifteen years. However, according to Hedaya (al-Marghinani 1982), the earliest age of majority for a boy is twelve years and for a girl it is nine years. As the contract of Islamic marriage insists on the free consent of the parties, only a person of sound mind can enter into marriage relationships.

MARRIAGES PERMITTED IN PRE-ISLAMIC ARABIA

In pre-Islamic Arabia, Arab idolaters recognized several kinds of union between men and women. It is important to be informed about these practices as this was the setting in which revolutionary ideas were introduced by the mission of Prophet Muhammad (pbuh). A summary is given below of the various kinds of marriages and the Islamic views on them.

- The permanent marriage-tie of one woman with one man by giving a dower to the wife. Islam accepted and continued this type of marriage subject to the Quranic provision for divorce under certain circumstances.

- The master marrying his female slaves. The Quran permitted masters to marry their female slaves in verses 4:3, 4:24, and 4:25, but imposed adherence to the contract of marriage.

- *Nikah al-Zainaah:* This form of marriage took place when a man captured a woman in a war and wanted to marry her. As a captive, she could not refuse. In this form of marriage, there was no recitation of *khutba* nor was any dower paid to such a wife. The Quran recognizes this form of marriage in 4:24 and the Quran refers to these women as "those whom your right hand possesses." However, Islamic law demands that in the cases of these women, there must be a proper Islamic marriage, thereby implying that consent is essential.

- *Zawaj-al-Badal* (Mutual Exchange of Wives): In this form of marriage, a man would ask another man to forgo his own wife in the other man's favor and receiving the other man's wife in exchange. There was no dower in this exchange of wives (Ali 1968–71). Some Hanafi jurists allowed this form of marriage provided the name *zawaj-al-badal* is not used and *mahr al-mithl* (proper dower) is paid (al-Asqalani 1301 AH). However, this practice is contrary to the teachings of the Quran.

- *Zawaj-al Istibda:* This form of marriage was a temporary marriage of a woman with another man. The husband permitted his wife to cohabitate with that other man until pregnancy by that man was clear. The husband would refrain from going near her until she conceived through that man (Ali 1968–71). This form of union had close similarity with the *niyoga* marriage of the Aryans in India. Islam disapproves of such union of nonhusband with another man's wife.

- Union of a number of men (less than 10) with a single woman: In this form of cohabitation, all the men having sex with one woman claimed the paternity of the child born to this woman. The woman giving birth to a child in such case, would call all the men who had sex with her and would declare that the child belonged to a particular man. This type of marriage had some similarity with the marriage of Draupadi with five Pandavas in the Mahabharat, an Indian epic. Islam disapproves of this form of marriage.

- Although not claimed as a marriage by pre-Islamic Arab idolaters, the paternity of a child of a prostitute, resulting from her promiscuous relationships with a number of men, was decided by a *qaif.* A *qaif* was one who was recognized as an expert to decide about the paternity of the child based on the similarity of features between a particular man and the child. The opinion of the *qaif* regarding the paternity of the child was accepted as proof of the child's paternity. Islam did not accept this custom of deciding the paternity of the child of a prostitute.

- *Nikah al-Dayzan:* Under this form of marriage, after the death of his father, the eldest son of the family was entitled to marry his father's wives. The son would exercise this right of the widow's deceased husband by throwing a cloth over her head, thus inheriting his father's wives. Upon the death of such a wife married under *nikah al-dayzan,* the son would inherit her wealth (Fida 1325 A. H.). Verses 4:19 and 4:22 of the Quran prohibited such a form of marriage.

- *Zawaj al-Shigar:* This form of marriage was like any other common form of marriage except for the fact that there was no dower. In this type of marriage, a man would marry his daughter or sister to a man who in turn, would marry his sister or daughter to the first mentioned man (Abu-Daud n.d.). This form of marriage is prohibited in Islam and the Prophet (pbuh) is reported to have remarked, "There is no *shigar* form of marriage in Islam." (Muslim n.d.). Despite this clear Hadith, some Hanafi jurists allow this form of marriage provided this name is not used and *mahr al-mithl* (proper dower) is paid (al-Asqalani 1301 AH).

- *Muta* Marriage: This was a form of marriage that permitted a temporary marriage for a specified period of time after which the *muta* marriage was automatically dissolved. This form of marriage is discussed in detail below.

Muta Marriage in Islamic Law

The Arabic word *muta* means 'profiting by' or 'enjoying a thing'. Through *muta* marriage, the Arab idolaters of pre-Islamic Arabia enjoyed a special right of temporary union with women. There is some confusion in the minds of ordinary Muslims and even among some scholars of Islamic law on the permissibility of *muta* marriage in Islam. However, through a proper consideration of the Quran, Hadith, and the opinions of the companions (*ashabs*) of the Prophet (pbuh), it is abundantly clear that *muta* marriage is not permitted in Islam.

The Quran, the primary source of Islamic law, does not mention or allow *muta* marriage. There is no mention of *muta* marriage having ever been allowed in the Hadith. In fact, many Hadiths show the Prophet (pbuh) ordered against the *muta* marriage on several occasions. These are given below.

- Ibn Abbas reported that Ali Ibn Abu Taleb had told him the Prophet (pbuh) had prohibited the *muta* marriage and the meat of domestic asses at the time of the Khaibar expedition (7AH) (B 67:32).

- Ali B. Abu Talib reported that the *muta* marriage was prohibited at the time of Umral Qadza (7AH) (B 64:40).

- *Muta* was prohibited at the time of the conquest of Mecca. (8 AH) (B 72:27).

- *Muta* was prohibited at the time of the Autas expedition. (9 AH) (B 72:27).

- *Muta* was prohibited at the time of the Tabuk expedition. (9 AH) (B 90:4).

- *Muta* was prohibited at the time of the Hujjatul Bida. (Farewell Pilgrimage) of the Prophet. (pbuh) (10 AH)

- Imam Muslim quotes some alleged Hadiths permitting *muta* marriage but admits that *muta* was finally prohibited by the Prophet (pbuh) (M 16:3). Imam Muslim further states that Caliph Umar I had to make a public declaration saying that *muta* was prohibited.

The only section of the Muslim community that accepts *muta* marriage is permitted by Islamic law is the Imamiyah subsect of the Ithna-Ashari Shiahs.

The Shiah translator of the Quran, Mir Ahmed Ali (1988) has argued *muta* marriage is permitted by Islamic law by quoting a relevant portion of 4:24. The relevant portion of 4:24 says, "*Famas tamtatum bihi minhunna faatu hunna ujurahunna faariztan.*" These words are translated by Yusuf Ali, Muhammad Ali, Muhammad Asad, and Mir Ahmed Ali in their respective translations of the Quran. These are given below.

- "Seeing that you derive benefit from them, give them their dowers (at least) as prescribed." (4:24—Yusuf Ali's translation)

- "Then as to those whom you profit (by marrying) give them their dowries as appointed." (4:24—Muhammad Ali's translation)

- "And unto those with whom you desire to enjoy marriage, you shall give the dowers due to them." (4:24—Muhammad Asad's translation)

- "And as such of them you had *muta* with, give them their dowries as a fixed reward." (4:24—Mir Ahmed Ali's translation)

It is clearly evident from the above that Mir Ahmed Ali's translation of the phrase "*Famas tamtatum bihi minhunna*" in 4:24 is a complete departure from the other translations of the same portion of 4:24, which always means, 'that you profit by,' 'derive benefit from,' or 'desire to enjoy.' The meaning of this expression as given by Mir Ahmed Ali is completely unacceptable. Apart from incorrectly translating the relevant portion of 4:24 as referring to *muta*, Mir Ahmed Ali (1988) writes when commenting on this verse, "Muta or a limited wedlock was allowed in Islam during the whole life time of the Prophet, during Abu Bakr's Caliphate and also for two or more years during Omar's Caliphate, but Omar prohibited it of his own accord against the sanction of the Quran. Ali renewed it and none thereafter prohibited it." However, neither the Hadith quoted above nor the relevant portion of 4:24 nor the history of early Islam supports the aforesaid comment of Mir Ahmed Ali.

Another Shiah lawyer and jurist, Sayyid Ameer Ali (1976) says, "It is declared to be abominable, though not actually prohibited, to marry in the *muta* form, a virgin who has no father, the reason being that as such a marriage is to her prejudice, and she has no paternal advice or guidance in the matter, she should not be subjected to the degradation of a temporary union." However, Ameer Ali could not quote any authority to support his claim that *muta* was not prohibited. The Hadiths quoted above also challenge the opinions of Mir Ahmed Ali and other Imamiyahs that Omar I was the first to prohibit *muta* and that Ali renewed it.

The Mutazalite jurist Zamakshari (1977) created some confusion by quoting contradictory authorities of Ibne Abbas and a questionable alleged Hadith. Zamakshari reports that Ibne Abbas used to recite "*Famas tamtatum bihi min hunna*" of 4:24 with the additional words, "*Ila ajalin musamma*" (take benefit of these women for a specified time). But Zamakshari also reports Ibne Abbas recanted his earlier stand and said before his death that *muta* was not permitted. It is worth noting that no Shia or Imamiyah authority agrees with the alleged earlier view of Ibne Abbas regarding the additional words in 4:24. Zamakshari also quoted an alleged Hadith of the Prophet (pbuh) wherein the Prophet (pbuh) is alleged to have said, "I had permitted you to practice *muta* but Allah has prohibited it till the Day of the Judgement." This alleged Hadith must be rejected as it contradicts 46:9 of the Quran that says, "Say: I am no bringer of new fangled doctrine among the apostles, nor do I know what will be done with me or with you. I follow but that which is revealed to me by inspiration. I am but a warner, open and clear." (46:9) Besides, this particular alleged Hadith quoted by Zamakshari also states Allah prohibited *muta*.

Muhammad Ali (1951), in his comment on 4:24 opines that Islamic law recognizes only *ihsan* (taking a woman in permanent marriage) and does not permit *muta* (temporary marriage). Ali further states that all sexual relationships outside *ihsan* are *musafihat* (giving oneself up to debauchery) or fornication and that no rights or obligations arise in *musafihat*. He also states *muta* was a form of temporary marriage which was recognized in pre-Islamic Arabia.

Concubinage in Islamic Law

Concubinage has been defined as a man's regular sexual relationship with a woman who has not the legal and social status of the wife of the man. In pre-Islamic Arabia concubinage was permitted with female slaves and with the female prisoners of war. The same custom was followed by some

Muslims until the revelation of the Quranic verses prohibiting concubinage. Following are the Quranic verses prohibiting concubinage.

- "Marry those among you who are single, or the virtuous ones among your slaves, male or female: if they are in poverty, God will give them means out of his grace: for God encompasses all, and He knows all things." (24:32)

  In this verse we find the same marriage instructions to master and mistress of female and male slaves. Therefore, there is no question of permitting concubinage of master with his female slave as mistresses are never allowed to have sex with their male slaves.

- "...but force not your maids to prostitution when they desire chastity, in order that you make a gain in the goods of this life. But if anyone compels them yet, after such compulsion, is God oft forgiving, most merciful [to them]." (24:33)

It is quite clear from 24:32 and 24:33 that if any master of a female slave kept her as his concubine after the revelation of these two verses, he was certainly violating Quranic injunctions against keeping female slaves as concubines. However, the unfortunate female slave who is compelled by her master to fornication will receive mercy from God. In his comment on 24:33, Muhammad Ali (1951) offers valuable historical information regarding using female slaves for prostitution in pre-Islamic Arabia and that despite the prohibition by 24:33 of such a practice, Abdullah Ibn Ubbay, the leader of the hypocrites, continued this bad practice. Furthermore, according to 4:3, 4:24, 4:25, 24:32, and 24:33, the precedent condition of a conjugal relationship with a female slave is marriage. However, the expressions "*Ma malakat yaminu-ku*" (what your (singular) right hand possesses) and "*Ma malakat aimanu-kum*" (what your (plural) right hands possess) in 23:5, 23:6, 24:31, 70:29, 70:30, 4:24, 4:25, 4:3, and 33:50 of the Quran has created confusion among Muslims and some jurists of Islamic law. Following are the relevant verses:

- "If you fear that you shall not be able to deal justly with the orphans, marry women of your choice, two or three or four; but if you fear that you will not be able to deal justly (with them), then only one, or (a captive) that your right hands possess . . . " (4:3)

- "If any of you have not the means wherewith to wed free believing women, they may wed believing girls from among those whom your right hands possess . . . " (4:25)

- "Also (prohibited are) women already married, except those whom your right hands possess . . . " (4:24)

- "The Believers must (eventually) win through—Those who humble themselves in their prayers; Who avoid vain talk; Who are active in deeds of charity; Who abstain from sex, except with those joined to them in the marriage bond, or (the captives) whom their right hands possess, for (in their case) they are free from blame." (23:5–6)

- " . . . and not display their beauty except to their husbands, their fathers, their husbands' fathers, their sons, theirs husbands' sons, their brothers or their brothers' sons, or their sisters' sons, or their women, or the slaves whom their right hands possess, or male servants free of physical needs, or small children who have no sense of the shame of sex . . . " (24:31)

- "O Prophet! We have made lawful to you your wives to whom you have paid their dowers; and those whom your right hand possesses out of the prisoners of war whom God has assigned to you . . . " (33:50)

- "And those who guard their chastity, except with their wives and the (captives) whom their right hands possess—for (then) they are not to be blamed." (70:29–30)

The expression in the Quran, "whom your right hand possesses," needs careful examination. Commenting on this expression, Abdullah Yusuf Ali (1946) says that 'those whom your right hand possesses' refers to captives of religious war, or wars led by rightly-guided leaders against the persecutors of faith. This is why, opines Yusuf Ali, the previous marriage of these female captives are dissolved and they become eligible for marriage with their Muslim captors. Yusuf Ali's opinion on this matter is supported by 4:24. While prohibiting Muslims to marry a woman who is already married, 4:24 excludes from this category 'those whom your right hand possesses' or captives of war who, even if married before captivity, can be married to a Muslim male. The verses 23:1–6 and 70:29–30 ask Muslims not to have sex with anybody except spouses and 'those whom your right hands possess' who, as explained earlier, are captives of war. Nowhere in the Quran is it mentioned that men can have sex with these women without marriage. The difference between other spouses and 'those whom your right hands possess' is the fact there is no obligation to pay dower to the latter category of women as mentioned in 33:50. Verse 33:50 allows the Prophet (pbuh), by way of exception, to keep all his existing wives (with rights of dower) and those prisoners as wives without the right of dower. Commenting on 33:50, Muhammad Ali (1951) informs us the Prophet (pbuh) himself lawfully married two prisoners of war, namely Saffiya, a Jewish woman, and Juwairiya, of the Bani Mustaliq tribe. The dowers of these two women were their freedom. The verse 24:31 gives a list of persons including 'whom their right hands possess,' before whom women are excused for displaying their beauty or their adornments. Persons whom their right hand possesses includes slaves, male or female.

Verse 4:25 asks Muslims to marry free believing women and believing girls from among those 'whom your right hands possess.' 4:3 also asks the Muslims to marry 'that which your right hands possess'.

From the above discussion it is clear that both *azwaj* (wives) and *Ma malakat yaminuka* (those whom your right hand possesses) are lawfully married wives and the difference between these two groups of wives is that the former were free women at the time of their marriage with rights of dower and the latter were prisoners of war at the time of marriage with no rights of dower.

In view of 4:3, 4:24, 4:25, 24:32, 70:30, and 24:33 those jurists of Islamic law who laid down the rule that a master may have sexual relationship with his female slaves without marriage are totally mistaken. The Quranic stand on this point is further strengthened by the Prophet's (pbuh) authentic Hadith opposing extra-marital sexual relationship of the master with his slave girls. The Hadith given below is found in all six collections of the *Siha Sitta*.

"There are three people for whom there is a double reward; a person belonging to *ahl-al-kitab* who believes in his own Prophet and believes in Muhammad; and the slave owned by another who fulfills his obligation towards Allah and his obligation towards his master; and the man who has a slave girl with him, then he teaches her good manners and instructs her well in polite accomplishments, and he educates her and gives her good education, then he sets her free and marries her; he has a double reward."
(B 3:31; 49:14, 16; 56:145; 60:48; 67:13) (M 16:14)(AD 12:5)

THE RULES OF *AKFA* AND MUSLIM MARRIAGE

The Arabic word *akfa* is the plural of *kuf* meaning an equal or one alike. For example, Arabs are the *akfa* (equal) of the Arabs, the Quraish are the *akfa* of the Quraish, and the member of one race, tribe, or family are *akfa* among themselves.

However, Islam, the leveler of all distinctions between societies, tribes, nations, races, and families did not and could not limit or restrict marriage relationships between men and women on the basis of *akfa*. The following verses of the Quran and historical facts will support the proposition that Islam is opposed to the *akfa* rules of marriage.

- "The Believers, men and women, are protectors, one of another: they enjoin what is just, and forbid what is evil: they observe regular prayers, practise regular charity, and obey God and His Messenger. On them will God pour His Mercy: for God is Exalted in power, Wise." (9:71)

- "The Believers are but a single Brotherhood: so make peace and reconciliation between your two (contending) brothers; and fear God, that you may receive Mercy." (49:10)

- "O mankind! We created you from a single (pair) of a male and a female, and made you into nations and tribes, that you may know each other (not that you may despise each other). Verily the most honoured of you in the sight of God is (he who is) the most righteous of you. And God has full knowledge and is well acquainted (with all things)." (49:13)

  The verse 49:13 was interpreted by the Prophet Muhammad (pbuh) in the following words: "The Arabs have no precedence over the nonArabs, nor the nonArabs over the Arabs, nor the white man over the black man, nor the black man over the white man except by excelling in righteousness." (Ali 1950)

- " . . . Except for these, all others are lawful, provided you seek (them in marriage) with gifts from your property—desiring chastity, not lust . . . " (4:24)

The following three historical facts show Islam's opposition to the *akfa* rules for marriages. The Prophet (pbuh) arranged the marriage of his cousin Zainab (a Quraish) with his liberated slave, Zaid. Hazrat Belal (although a Sahaba) was a negro and a liberated slave. He was married to the sister of an Arab Sahaba, Abdur Rahman Ibne Auf. The Prophet (pbuh) recommended Abu Hind (a Hajania and his liberated slave) to the tribe of Bani Bayadz saying "O Bani Bayadz! Give (your daughter) to Abu Hind in marriage and take in marriage his (Abu Hind's) daughters." (AD 12:26)

Despite the aforesaid authorities against *akfa* in the matter of Islamic marriages, the conservative jurists of Shariah insisted upon *akfa* in marriages and the majority of them stressed the need of *akfa* in four things, namely religion, freedom, descent, and profession before entering into a marriage relationship. However, the absence of *akfa* has been excused by Imam Shafii and Imam Malik. Imam Shafii (n.d.) states that a marriage outside *akfa* is not prohibited by Islam as the consent of the bride and that of her guardian remove the disability on account of the lack of *akfa*. Imam Malik (1981) was of the opinion that equity is brought about by religion and all Muslims are alike or equal.

The Quran categorically and clearly opposes *akfa* in the following verse, "…(Lawful unto you in marriage) are (not only) chaste women who are believers, but chaste women among the people of the book, revealed before your time—when you give them their due dowers, and desire chastity, not lewdness, nor secret intrigues…" (5:6) In another verse, the Quran permits marriage with partners who are poor, thereby opposing *akfa*. The verse states, "…if they are in poverty, God will give them means out of His Grace…" (24:32)

INDEPENDENCE OF WOMEN TO MARRY WITHOUT A GUARDIAN

The Quran and the Hadith confer the right of independence to a Muslim woman to enter into a marriage contract without the interference of the marriage guardian. However, on the plea of the bashfulness of Muslim virgins and on the false pretence of helping women in the choice of their husbands because of their alleged inexperience, male dominated Muslim society, conservative theologians, and the jurists of Islam imposed the institution of guardianship for the marriage of Muslim virgins, both adult and minor. The following verses of the Quran and the following Hadiths clearly recognize the rights of adult Muslim women to enter into a marriage contract without the interference of a guardian.

- "And when you divorce women, and they fulfill the terms of their (iddat) don't prevent them from marrying their (former) husbands, if they mutually agree on equitable terms…" (2:232)

    This verse refers directly to marriage between a divorced woman and her former husband, which is clearly allowed by this verse, without going through the mock ceremony of marriage with another person. Verse 2:232 was revealed when the sister of Maqil bin Yasir was divorced by her husband when the *iddat* was over and then the husband approached Maqil's sister to marry him again. She agreed but Maqil did not. The Prophet (pbuh) allowed the marriage of Maqil's sister to her former husband despite the opposition of Maqil to this union (B 65:40). However this verse may also apply to the marriage of a divorced woman with another person without the permission of a marriage guardian.

- " . . . But if they (the widows) leave (the residence) there is no blame on you for what they do with themselves provided it is reasonable. And God is Exhalted in Power, Wise." (2:240)

  Reasonable deeds of the widows mentioned in this verse also include their lawful deeds of marriage. Therefore, from this verse it is clear that the widows can marry lawfully without the permission of their marriage guardians.

Two Hadiths collected by Abu Daud (n.d.) support the view that widows and divorced women can marry without interference from their marriage guardians. They are the following:

- "The widow or the divorced woman has greater right to dispose of herself in marriage than her guardian."

- "The guardian has no business in the matter of the divorced woman or the widow."

Let us now consider the position of a virgin with regards to her rights of marriage without the interference of their guardians. According to the Hanafi school of law, "The marriage contract of a free woman who has reached the age of majority and is possessed of understanding, is complete with her own consent, whether she is a virgin or has been married before, though it may not have been confirmed by her guardian" (al-Marghinani 1982). Ameer Ali (1976) opines that according to the Shia view, no guardian is required in the marriage of an adult female. Both Malik and Shafii believe that the consent of the guardian is essential. According to a Hadith in Sahih Bukhari, "The father or any other guardian cannot give in marriage a virgin or one who has been married before without her consent." (B 67:42). According to a Hadith by Ibn Abbas, "a virgin girl came to the Prophet (pbuh) and said that her father had married her against her wishes and the Prophet (pbuh) gave her right to repudiate her marriage" (AD 12:25). Bukhari's Sahih contains another Hadith that says that the Prophet (pbuh) repudiated the marriage of a woman solemnized by her guardian without her consent.

CHILD MARRIAGE IN ISLAMIC LAW

While discussing the essentials of Islamic marriage, we observe that as a contract, an Islamic marriage can only be entered by persons of marriageable age (i.e., one who has attained majority). There is no record of any marriage of a minor through his or her guardian allowed by the Prophet (pbuh) after the details of the laws regarding the marriage of orphans were revealed at Medina by the Quranic verse 4:6. The Prophet's (pbuh) own marriage to Ayesha when she was nine years old was performed in Mecca long before the Islamic laws of marriage were revealed at Medina by the Quranic verses. However as the consummation of the said marriage of Ayesha and the Prophet (pbuh) was postponed for five years (some say seven years) to allow Ayesha to attain majority, in reality the marriage of Ayesha took place when she was either 14 or 16 years old.

Although there is nothing in the Quran about child marriage, pre-Islamic Arab customs that allowed child marriage played a major role in introducing child marriage to Islam. Besides, there are some Hadiths that refer to child marriage. The Shariah, therefore, permits child marriage of both sexes. As minors cannot enter into a contract of marriage on their own, it is logical that marriages of minors could be contracted, on their behalf, by their guardians. By the rules of all schools of law, marriage guardians have the power to give children of both sexes in marriage without their consent, until they reach the age of puberty (*bulugh*) or majority. The Hanafi law insists that the marriage guardian must be the minor's *asaba* (relations on the father's side). This law was modified slightly to allow the mother or maternal relations to become marriage guardians in the absence of *asaba* agnates, although the position of mothers, or maternal relations on the ladder of marriage guardians is very close to the bottom. According to Ameer Ali (1976), the following persons are entitled, in order of priority, to act as a marriage guardian: (1) the father, (2) father's father, (3) the brother and other collaterals according to the priorities in the law of inheritance, (4) the mother and maternal relations, and (5) the ruling authority (i.e., the *kazi* or the court). The Maliki law gives a woman no right to become a marriage guardian and recognizes only the father as a marriage guardian. The Shafii law gives the right of marriage guardian either to the father or to the grandfather. The marriage guardian's power of imposing the status of marriage (*jabr*) continues, under the Hanafi or Ithna Ashari Shia law, until the child attains the age of puberty. Upon attaining majority (*bulugh*), erstwhile minors have the right of the '*khiyar al-bulugh*' (option of puberty). By exercising this right, he or she can repudiate the marriage contracted on their behalf while they were minors. If the girl was not married during her minority, on attaining the age of puberty she can, according to the Hanafi or Ithna Ashari law, marry without a guardian. According to the Maliki, Shafii, Fatimid Shias, Daudi, or Sulaymani Bohras, the marriage guardian's power of *jabr* continues over women until they are married and emancipated from parental control. Therefore, they cannot marry without a guardian even after attaining majority.

It should be noted that all the innovative rules of child marriage introduced by the various schools of Muslim law are not as fundamental as the Quranic injunctions or the injunctions of the Hadith. Therefore, Muslims of modern times, by the exercise of *ijtihad*, can change these rules if the needs of modern society demand it. Some changes in this area of law have been made on the Indian subcontinent and in other countries in the twentieth century. The Dissolution of Muslim Marriages Act 1939 has made some reform in the laws of the khiyar al-bulugh for all Muslim minors in India, Pakistan, and Bangladesh. The Muslim Family Law Ordinance 1961 made further reforms in the law of the khiyar al-bulugh for all Muslim minors in Pakistan and in Bangladesh.

POLYGAMOUS MARRIAGE IN ISLAMIC LAW

Generally speaking, Islamic law recognizes monogamy or the union of one man and one woman as a valid form of marriage. However Islamic law also allows polygamy under exceptional circumstances. The conditions for polygamy are dealt with by the following verses of the Quran, which are also relevant for treatment towards the orphans.

- "O mankind! Reverance your Guardian-Lord, who created you from a single person, created of like nature his mate . . . " (4:1)

- "To orphans restore their property (when they reach their age), nor substitute (your) worthless things for (their) good ones; and devour not their substance (by mixing it up) with your own. For this is indeed a great sin.

If you fear that you shall not be able to deal justly with the orphans, marry women of your choice, two, or three, or four; but if you fear that you shall not be able to deal justly (with them), then only one, or (a captive) that your right hands possess. That will be more suitable, to prevent you from doing injustice." (4:2–3)

- "They ask your instruction concerning the women. Say: God does instruct you about them: and (remember) what has been rehearsed to you in the Book, concerning the orphans of women to whom you don't give the portions prescribed, and yet whom you desire to marry, as also concerning the children who are weak and oppressed; that you stand firm for justice to orphans. There is not a good deed which you do but God is well acquainted therewith." (4:127)

- "You are never able to be fair and just as between women, even if it is your ardent desire: but turn not away (from a woman) alto-gether, so as to leave her (as it were) hanging (in the air). If you come to friendly understanding, and practice self-restraint, God is oft forgiving, Most Merciful." (4:129)

Verses 4:3 and 4:127 have been critically examined and analyzed in light of the history surrounding the revelation of these verses. Various Islamic theologians and jurists have given their considered opinions re-garding the real implications of these verses. Following is a summary of these opinions. Verse 4:3 must be read in conjunction with verses 4:1 and 4:2. Verse 4:1 stresses the equality of the sexes by pointing out the cre-ation of men and women from the same source. Verse 4:2 asks Muslims to give orphans their property and not to substitute their good property with worthless property of the guardians of the orphans. Verse 4:3 urges Muslims to do justice to orphans and permits polygamy (marrying two, three, or four women) only if there is apprehension of not doing justice to the orphans. On the other hand, if Muslims feel they cannot do justice to the orphans by marrying more than one wife they must marry only one wife. The permission to marry 'that which your right hand possesses' meaning slave women, is irrelevant today due to the absence of slavery in modern society. The expression 'women' in 4:3 refers to the mothers of the orphans and as 4:127 refers to the rule in 4:3 ('what has been re-hearsed unto you in the Book') it supports the contention that 4:3 refers to the mothers of the orphans ('concerning the orphans of the women' 4:127) as well as to the orphans themselves. Hazrat Aisha understood 4:3 as meaning that if the guardians of orphan girls feared that they could not do justice to the orphans by marrying them, then they should marry other women (quoted in the Sahih Muslim). It is therefore clear that the emphasis is doing justice to the orphans rather than marrying more than one woman. Differing slightly from the interpretation of 4:3 by Aisha, a *tabeyun* (successor of the *sahabas*), Said Ibn Jabayr states the following about the message of 4:3, "Just as you are, rightly, fearful of offending against the interest of orphans, you must apply the same consideration to the interests and rights of women whom you intend to marry." (Asad 1984) It is clear from the above discussion of 4:1–3 and 4:127 that the permission for polygamy in these verses of the Quran was revealed in the context of orphan girls and their property.

All the *mufassirs* (commentators of the Quran) agree that the fourth chapter (*sura*), particularly these verses, were revealed immediately after the Battle of Uhud, to guide Muslims when, due to the martyrdom of about ten percent of Muslim males during the battle, the number of women was much greater than the number of men. According to Muhammad Ali (1951) the Quranic permission given to Muslim males to have more than one wife was given under these peculiar circumstances of Muslim society having a considerably reduced male population. This permission given to Muslim males to marry orphans and their widowed mothers was conditional on doing justice to all of them and particularly in relation to their property. The *Mutazilite mufassir*, Zamakhshari (1977), opined that God had given permission for polygamy only in cases of orphan girls and their guardians. The guardians have the option to marry their wards if they cannot resist the temptation to misappropriate their wards' property. This is treated as a lesser evil by the Quran. Thus according to Zamakhshari, the permission for polygamy is not a general license and therefore all Muslim males do not have permission to marry up to four wives. Verse 4:129 makes it more difficult for a Muslim to fulfill the conditions of polygamy as it categorically states one cannot do justice between wives even if one so wishes. Relying on this interpretation of 4:129, *Mutazilite* theologians opine that the condition of treating wives equally cannot be fulfilled. Therefore polygamy is as good as banned. Muhammad Asad (1984) suggests that 4:129 be read in conjunction with 4:3, particularly the concluding part, which imposes a moral restriction on plural marriage. In the late nineteenth century the Egyptian theologian and Islamic jurist, Mohammad Abduh, declared that the current regulations of Islamic Shariah regarding polygamy did not belong to the essentials of Islam, but were subject to modifications according to needs and circumstances (Engineer 1992).

The abuse of permission for restricted polygamy has been remedied by various Muslim countries. By interpreting 4:3 through *qiyas*, Tunisia has outlawed polygamy completely. However Turkey's prohibition on polygamy has nothing to do with Islamic law as on this matter Turkey adopted Roman-Dutch law in substitution for Islamic law. Moroccan law declares, "If any injustice is to be feared between co-wives, polygamy is not permitted." The Moroccan courts are allowed to intervene retrospectively by granting judicial divorce to a wife who complains of injury suffered as a result of her husband contracting a second marriage. In this sphere, Moroccan lawmakers have reformed the traditional Islamic Shariah by *ijtihad*. Reformed Iraqi law demands that there must be the additional requirement of some lawful benefit resulting from a polygamous marriage and the Iraqi court has discretion to refuse permission to a polygamous marriage "if any failure of equal treatment between co-wives is feared." By their statutes and ordinance, Syria, Iraq, Pakistan, and Bangladesh require official permission for a polygamous marriage. In Syria the *qazis* have the right to refuse permission for a polygamous marriage if the husband is not in a position to maintain and support more than one wife. In Pakistan and Bangladesh, the Muslim Family Law Ordinance 1961 authorizes the Arbitration Council, consisting of the chairman of the local Union Council, a representative of the husband, and a representative of the existing wife to give necessary permission or not for a polygamous marriage. The Arbitration Council will arrive at their decision on the basis of whether it is "satisfied that the proposed polygamous marriage is necessary, just, and subject to conditions, if any, as may be deemed fit." A second marriage without the permission of the Arbitration Council is not invalid but the 1961 Ordinance makes the husband liable for imprisonment up to one year, a fine up to 5000 rupees/takas, or both. In addition, if the husband does not have permission for a polygamous marriage from the Arbitration Council he will have to pay, forthwith, the entire dower to his existing wife even if it was deferred and the existing wife will have a right of judicial dissolution of her marriage.

MARRIAGE OF MUSLIMS WITH NON-MUSLIMS IN ISLAMIC LAW

The following Quranic verses are relevant for this topic.

- "And marry not the idolatresses until they believe; and certainly a believing maid is better than a idolatress even though she please you. Nor give (believing women) in marriage to idolaters until they believe, and certainly a believing slave is better than an idolater, even though he please you. These invite to the fire and God invites to the garden and to forgiveness by His will and He makes clear His messages to men that they may be mindful." (2:221—translation of Muhammad Ali)

- "This day are (all) things good and pure made lawful unto you. The food of the people of the book is lawful unto you and yours is lawful unto them. (Lawful unto you in marriage) are (not only) chaste women who are believers, but chaste women among the People of the Book, revealed before your time—when you give them their dowers, and desire chastity, not lewdness, nor secret intrigues. If anyone rejects faith, fruitless is his work and in the hereafter he will be in the ranks of those who have lost (all spiritual good)." (5:6)

- "Verily We have sent you in truth, as a bearer of glad tidings, and as a warner: and there never was a people, without a warner having lived among them (in the past)." (35:24)

- "Or do they say, 'he has forged it?' Nay, it is the truth from your Lord, that you may admonish a people to whom no warner has come before you: in order that they may receive guidance." (32:3)

- "In order that you may admonish a people, whose fathers had received no admonition, and who therefore remained heedless (of the sign of God)." (36:6)

The questions dealt with in 2:221 of the Quran arose in connection with warfare. The previous verse speaks of orphans whose numbers were no doubt greatly increased by the wars. This verse deals with intermarriages with idolaters. The war with the idolaters, who were now not a people differing in religious views only but enemies bent upon the destruction of the Muslims, had brought new conditions into force. Intermarriages with those who were waging war upon the Muslims could have led to serious trouble and numerous complications. A reference to 60:10 will show that even the marital relationships already existing between believing women and their unbelieving husbands had to be ended on account of the war. Hence the prohibition of such intermarriages.

Looking at 2:221 in detail it should be noted that the prohibition to marry mentioned in this verse relates to idolatresses and idolaters and not to unbelievers in general as Abdullah Yusuf Ali translates. So far as the accuracy of the translation of 2:221 is concerned, Muhammad Ali seems to be more accurate than Abdullah Yusuf Ali, and Muhammad Ali correctly translated the words '*mushrakatay*' and '*mushraykina*' as idolatresses and idolaters, respectively. The accuracy of these translations of these two words in 2:221 is important because it is necessary to know exactly to whom the prohibition relates. We should take special care to notice that the Quranic prohibition regarding marrying non-Muslim men and women mentioned in 2:221 relates to idolaters and not to unbelievers generally.

In his comment on 5:6, Muhammad Ali (1951) observes that marriage of a Muslim man with a woman whose religion is based on a revealed book (who are found in almost all nations of the world), is permissible. Ali states that on the question of Muslim women marrying men among the *ahlil kitab* (people of the revealed book) the Quran is silent, and from the earliest times, Muslims were against it. He also points out the companions of the Prophet (pbuh) extended the law to accept Parsis as *ahlil kitab*. Verse 5:6 permits Muslim men to marry women from among 'the people of the book' (*ahlil kitab*). In view of the Quran specifically mentioning the Torah (*Taurat* or the Book of Moses), the Gospel (*Injil* or the book of Jesus) in many verses, and the Psalms of David (*Zabur*) in 17:55, the jurists of Islam are unanimous in accepting Jews and Christians as 'the people of the book' (*ahlil kitab*).

The Quran says "Those who believe (in the Quran), those who follow the Jewish (scriptures), and the Sabians and the Christians—any who believe in God and the Last Day, and work righteousness—on them shall be no fear, nor they shall they grieve" (5.72). The same message is repeated with slight variation in 2:62 of the Quran. From these two verses it is presumed that the Quran accepts the Jews, the Christians, and the Sabians as *ahlil kitab*. The status of the Sabians is further strengthened by *The Hedaya* (al-Marghinani 1982) says, "And it is lawful to marry Sabian women if they profess a religion and accept a revealed book, for they are among *ahl-al-kitab*."

According to some Muslim jurists Christians are idolaters as they accept Jesus Christ as God or as the Son of God. However this opinion of the jurists of Islam is untenable in view of the emphatic declaration of the Quran that the Christians are *ahlil kitab* despite the Quran criticizing the Christians for accepting Jesus Christ as God or Son of God. In view of this discussion it appears that the Quran permits a Muslim man to marry a woman from among the people of the Book irrespective of whether a particular section of the *ahlil kitabis* are idolaters as well. In view of this it is possible Hindus, Sikhs, Jains, Parsis, Buddhists, Taoists, Confucians and the Magians can be considered *ahlil kitab*, as all these religious groups have scriptures, and despite the fact that some of these groups are idolaters. Verse 35:24 states that every people had a warner and although the Quran specifically mentions of only four *kitabs*, namely, the Quran, the *Torah*, the *Injil* and the *Zabur* it is not an exhaustive list. There may be many other Books of God which were revealed through the warners of these people. Verses 32:3 and 36:6 mention that Arab idolaters and idolatresses had no warner before the Prophet Muhammad (pbuh). These two verses lead us to the conclusion only Arab idolaters and idolatresses, who are mentioned in 2:221, are excluded from a matrimonial relationship with a Muslim.

With regard to a Muslim woman's capacity to marry men from among the *ahlil kitabis* both the Quran and the Hadith are silent. Although practice from the earliest time is against such unions, there is no reason to accept such views of the Muslim jurists on the principle of equality of the rights of men and women so far as the marriage partners are concerned. In fact, unions of Muslim women with *ahlil kitabi* men are supported by Verse 2:29 and the juristic principle of *ibaha*. Verse 2:29 of the Quran says, "It is He who hath created for you all things that are on earth…" The juristic principle of *ibaha* says, '*Al-ibaha asl-unfil-Aashya*' or 'lawfulness is recognized principle in all things' (Ahmed 133A.H.). In view of the above, it is an acceptable proposition that Islamic law permits marriage between Muslim men and Muslim women with women and men, respectively, belonging to the *ahlil kitab*, thus permitting marriage of a Muslim (both male and female) with persons of the opposite sex among the *ahlil kitabis*. The expression *ahlil kitab* means anybody who professes a religion and accepts a revealed book, which came before the Quran. Although controversial, this proposition has an enormous impact on Muslims in the global world of the new millennium. Today it is inevitable that more and more people will meet others from other faiths. Marriages will of course be a result. The basis for the acceptance of these interfaith marriages does exist within Islamic law. It remains to be seen whether this acceptance will occur in practice.

6

The Position of Husband and Wife in Islamic Law

Islamic law has always upheld the rights of Muslim women. The Quran and the Hadith are particularly concerned with the husbands' treatment of their wives. The Prophet Muhammad (pbuh) was extremely sympathetic to Muslim women and was conscious about the special rights of Muslim wives in matrimonial relationships with their husbands. The following Hadiths are eloquent testimony to the Prophet's (pbuh) attitude towards women and show clearly the Prophet (pbuh) wanted women to have as much equality with men as was possible in the male dominated and antiwomen Arab society of the seventh century A.D.

- "The most excellent of you is he who is best in the treatment of his wife." (M 13:11)

- "Everyone of you is a ruler and everyone shall be questioned about his subjects; the Amir (king) is a ruler and the man is a ruler over the people of his house, and the woman is a ruler over the house of her husband and his children; so everyone of you is a ruler, and everyone shall be questioned about his/her subjects." (B 67:91)

- "O my people! You have certain rights over your wives and your wives over you . . . They are the trust of God in your hands. So you must treat them with kindness." (M 15:19)

- "And be careful of your duty to God in the matter of women, for you have taken them as the trust of God . . . and they owe you this

49

obligation that they will not allow anyone whom you do not like to come into your home; if they do this, chastise them in such a manner that it should not leave any effect on their bodies." (M 15:19, T 10:11)

As the Quran is the most important authority for any Islamic rule on any matter, the Quranic verses on this topic are worth mentioning. The two Quranic verses that are most important for this topic are 4:34 and 2:228.

"Ar-rejalu qawwaamuna alaan nisaa-i bimaa fazzalal laahu baazahum alaa bazin wa bimaa aanfaquu min amwalihim. Fas-saalihaatu qaanitaatun haafi-zaatul-lil-gaibay bimaa hafizallah. Wallaatii takhaa funna nushuu zahunna faeezuuhunna wah-juruuhunna fil mazaaji-i wazribuu hunna faa-in ataa nakum falaa tabguu alayhinna sabilaan. Innallaha kaana aliyyan kabiraa." (4:34)

"Men are the protectors and maintainers of women, because God has given the one more (strength) than the other, and because they support them from their means. Therefore the righteous women are devoutly obedient and guard in (the husband's) absence what God would have them guard. As to those women on whose part you fear disloyalty and ill-conduct, admonish them (first); (next), refuse to share their beds, (and last) beat them (lightly); but if they return to obedience, seek not against them means (of annoyance): for God is Most High, Great (above you all). (4:34—translation of Yusuf Ali)

"Men are the maintainers of women, with what Allah has made some of them to excel others and with what they spend out of their wealth. So the good women are obedient, guarding the unseen as Allah has guarded. And as to those on whose part you feared desertion, admonish them, and leave them alone in the bed and chastise them. So if they obey you, seek not a way against them. Surely Allah is ever Exalted, Great." (4:34—translation of Muhammad Ali)

" . . . *wa lahunna mislullazii alaihinna bil maaruf: wa bir-rijaali alaihinna darajahtun. Wallaahu Aziizun Haakim."* (2:228)

"And women shall have rights similar to the rights against them, according to what is equitable; but men have a degree (of advan-

tage) over them. And God is Exalted in Power, Wise." (2:228—
translation of Yusuf Ali)

"...and women have rights similar to those against them in a
just manner, and men are a degree above them. And Allah is
Mighty, Wise." (2:228—translation of Muhammad Ali)

The various sections of 4:34 need to be examined very closely and the
comments of various interpreters of the Quran on these sections need to
be considered. The first section of 4:34 to be considered is *"Ar-rejalu
qawwaamuna alaan nisaa-i."* Lane (1980) translates it as "Men are the
maintainers of women and manage their affairs." Adopting Lane's translation, Muhammad Ali (1951) opines that as the maintainer of the wife,
the husband has final say in the affairs of the house and exercises authority over the wife whenever needed. Translating the word *'qawwaamuna,'*
Yusuf Ali (1946) says that it means "one who stands firm in another's
business, protects his interests and looks after his affairs or standing firm
in his own business." Zamakshari (1977) translates *'qawwaamuna alaan
nisaa-i'* as "men are the managers of the affairs of women." Pickthall
(1977) translates *'qawwaamuna'* as "in charge of." None of the above
authors speak of the superiority of men over women. However, the expo-
nent of conservative theology, Maudoodi (1958), says this expression means
that because God made men superior over women, men are the managers
of women's affairs. On the other extreme of the spectrum, Azizah-al-
Hibri (1982) rejects the translation of this section, which says men are
protectors and maintainers of women. According to al-Hibri, the basic
notion of 4:34 is moral guidance and caring. She criticizes the male
establishment for using 4:34 for their claim of divinely ordained, inherent,
superiority, and absolute authority over women. Azizah-al-Hibri opines
that only in extreme cases, such as insanity, do Muslim women lose their
right of self-determination. Interpreting *'qawwaamuna alaan nisaa-i'* in
4:34, Saiyyid Qutb (1980) restricts its meaning to the relationship between husband and wife. According to Qutb, the male partner's privilege
of being *'qawwaamuna'* or in charge of the affairs of the female partner
is due to the fact that the male provides for the female. Parvez (1979)
opposes Maudoodi's concept of superiority of men over women and says
the matrimonial relationship of husband and wife is not one of superiority
of one over the other, but one of camaraderie (*rafaqat*). According to
Parvez, *'qawwam'* in this context means nothing more than a provider of
the family. Both Umar Ahmad Usmani (1980) and Riffat Hassan interpret *'qawwam'* as managers. According to Usmani and Hassan, the Quran

in 4:34 states it is the husband's responsibility to maintain his wife and to be the breadwinner when the wife is bringing up the child. Usmani further opines that except for compensating the wife for looking after the children, the husband has no other superiority over his wife. Following Riffat Hassan, Engineer (1992) opines that in normal times (i.e. when the wives are not bearing children), wives may be breadwinners and then husbands no longer have superiority over their wives. Engineer further states the Quran never says men should be '*qawwam*' over women but that men are *qawwam* over women.

The next section of 4:34 states "*bimaa fazzalal laahu baazahum alaa bazin wa bimaa aanfaquu min amwalihim*" meaning "with what God has made some of them to excel over others with what they spend out of their wealth." This particular section of 4:34 has raised a serious question as to whether God prefers the husband to the wife. Expressing a pronounced antiwomen view, Zamakshari (1977) believes God has preferred men to women in terms of intelligence, physical constitution, determination, and physical strength. It is significant that Zamakshari fails to support his extreme view with any Quranic verse, Hadith, or any other acceptable authority. Contradicting Zamakshari's view on this point, Saiyyid Qutb (1980), a modern translator and interpreter of the Quran, states that the distinction between men and women is in their primordial nature (*fitrah*) and this distinction has no inherent value. It should be noted this section does not say that men are preferred, but that preference of some of them (men) over others (women) is because they (men) support them (women) from their means. In fact, in this section of 4:34 the common pronoun '*hum*' applying to both men and women is used. Finally, a cogent argument against men's superiority over women based on the language of 4:34, is supplied by Umar Ahmad Usmani (1980). He points out the wording of this section does not at all indicate men's superiority over women and had God desired to give superiority to men, He would have said in 4:34, '*bimaa fazzala hum alai hinna*' meaning 'He made them (men) superior to them (women)'.

The third section of 4:34 needing attention is "*Fas-saalihaatu qaanitaatun haafi-zaatul-lil-gaibay bimaa hafizallah*" meaning, "So the good women are obedient, guarding the unseen as Allah has guarded." Abdullah Yusuf Ali (1946), commenting on this section of 4:34, states that the Quran in 4:34 says the good wife should be obedient and harmonious not only in her husband's presence but in his absence should guard her husband's reputation, property, and her own religious duty as asked by God. Maulana Abul Kalam Azad (1980) translates this section in the same manner as Yusuf Ali and translates it as "carefully protecting in their (husband's) absence what God would have them protect." There is a great deal of controversy over the meaning of the expression '*qaanitaatun.*' It is translated as 'dutiful' by Maulana Azad (1980), 'devoutly obedient' by Yusuf Ali (1946), and as 'obedient' by Muhammad Marmaduke Pickthall (1977). However, the difficult question to answer relates to the very authority to which good women should be obedient. Various commentators of the Quran give different answers to this question. Zamakshari (1977) opines that the obedience referred to here means both obedience to God as well as obedience to the husband. However, his preferred meaning is obedience to husband. Ar-Razi says that *qaanitaatun* means obedience to husband (Engineer 1992). Mir Ahmed Ali (1988) opines that it means obedience to God and to nobody else. With respect, I submit that since the exact translation of the word '*qaanitaatun*' literally is 'obedience,' it should refer to 'obedience to God' as this is the main emphasis of Quranic teaching. It is interesting to note Verse 60:12 of the Quran never mentions obedience to the husband as one of the criterion for a believing woman.

The fourth section of 4:34 reads "*Wallaatii takhaa funna nushuu zahunna faeezuuhunna wah-juruuhunna fil mazaaji-i wazribuu hunna*" meaning "As to those women on whose part you fear disloyalty and ill-conduct, admonish them (first); (next), refuse to share their beds, (and last) beat them (lightly)." The first part of this section refers to the '*nushuz*' (disloyalty and ill-conduct) of the wife. Muhammad Ali (1951) translates '*nushuz*' as desertion or rising and he adds that when '*nushuz*' is used regarding a woman in relation to her husband it means 'her rising against her husband.' According to Imam Murtada (n.d.) '*nushuz*' of a woman means that she resists her husband, she hates him, and deserts him. Imam Ahmed Ibne Hanbal (1306 AH) thought that '*nushuz*' of a woman takes place when she leaves her husband's place of residence and starts living in a place her husband dislikes. Abu Bakr Jasas opines that '*nushuz*' applicable to a woman arises when she thinks and behaves as superior to her husband (Engineer 1992). According to Maulana Usmani (1980), '*nashaza*' means to rise from a place and '*nushuz*' of a woman refers to her breech of sexual conduct, her arrogance and taking advantage of her husband, and not to ordinary household quarrels. A husband's remedy for his wife's '*nushuz*,' as referred to in 4:34, is summarized by Imam Razi (n.d.). Razi states that at first a wife is admonished (*faeezuuhunna*) and if she desists, the evil is mended. If a wife persists in the wrong course, the husband refuses to share the bed (*wah-juruuhunna*). If she still persists, the last resort according to Razi is chastisement or beating (*wazribuu hunna*).

The ultimate remedy to a wife's 'nushuz' at her husband's disposal is 'wazribuu hunna'. While the majority of translators of the Quran translate 'wazribuu hunna' as 'beat them' (the wives), this translation is not accepted by some translators of the Quran. Both the Lisanul Arab and the Arabic-English Lexicon (Lane 1980) agree that 'zaraba' does not necessarily indicate force or violence. Raghib (1485) says that 'zaraba' metaphorically means not to have intercourse. Following Raghib's opinion, Mir Ahmed Ali (1988) translates 'wazribuu hunna' as meaning "don't go to bed with them (wives)." Among those translators who translate 'wazribuu' as meaning 'beating' Yusuf Ali (1946), Maulana Abul Kalam Azad (1980), and Zamakshari (1977) recommend beating lightly. Azad translates it as 'beating' but adds in parenthesis, 'without harming them.' While translating it as 'beating,' Zamakshari adds "it (beating) should be such as not to cause injury." He also quotes a Hadith in his support, which states, "Don't beat your subordinates as God's power over you is much greater than your power over your subordinates."

Before using the remedy of 'zaraba' (beating) for a wife's 'nushuz' one should be reminded of five matters regarding this particular remedy. First, 'zaraba' is a mere permission in extreme cases and neither a blanket permission nor an order to the husband. Second, the 'nushuz' of the husband is also mentioned in the Quran in 4:128 and there the recommended remedy is different. Verse 4:128 says, "If a wife fears from her husband cruelty (nushuzan) or desertion (eeraazan), there is no blame on them if they arrange an amicable settlement and such settlement is best . . . " On the basis of the wife's remedy for her husband's 'nushuz' prescribed by 4:128, it can be argued that the husband should have the same remedy for his wife's 'nushuz'. Third, the provision of arbitration for conjugal disputes mentioned in 4:35 and 4:128 is an alternative remedy. Fourth, although 'zaraba' (beating) is permitted in extreme cases for a wife's 'nushuz,' the traditions of the Prophet (pbuh) are against the practice of beating. The following Hadiths and historical incidents from the Prophet's (pbuh) life show that the Prophet (pbuh) discouraged beating for a wife's 'nushuz':

- "The best of you is he who is best to his wife."

- "You have a right in the matter of your wives that they do not allow anyone whom you don't like to come to your houses. If they do this, chastise them in such a manner that it should not leave an impression." (T 10:11)

- "On some women's complaints against their husbands' ill treatment of them, the Prophet (pbuh) said, 'You will not find these men as the best among you.'" (AD 12:42)

- Ibn Sa'd (n.d.) reported that the Prophet (pbuh) never raised his hands against anyone of his wives nor against a slave, nor against any person at all and the Prophet (pbuh) was always against the beating of women.

- Ibn Sa'd (n.d.) reported that on hearing complaints from men about the sowing of disorders by their wives, the Prophet (pbuh) said, "Very well, beat them, but only the worst among you will have recourse to such methods" and then he added, "I cannot bear seeing quick tempered men beating their wives in a fit of anger."

- Only on one occasion did the Prophet (pbuh) stay away from his wives for twenty-nine nights as being angry with them, he had declared that he would be away from home for a month but God had censored him for this. (Tabari 1967–69)

The following Quranic verses demonstrate the Quranic prescriptions of kind treatment of wives by their husbands:

- " . . . on the contrary live with them (the wives) on the footing of kindness and equity.
    If you take a dislike to them, it may be that you dislike a thing, and God brings about through it a great deal of good." (4:19)

- "A divorce is only permissable twice, after that the parties should either hold together on equitable terms, or separate with kindness . . . " (2:229)

- "When you divorce women, and they fulfil the terms of their (iddat) either take them back on equitable terms, or set them free on equitable terms . . . " (2:231)

In view of these Quranic verses and the attitude of the Prophet (pbuh) towards women, the prescription of 'nushuz' in 4:34 should be applied only in extreme circumstances and when all other remedies fail. Furthermore, the Quranic remedies for a husband's 'nushuz' (mentioned in 4:128) may also be considered as the proper remedy for a wife's 'nushuz' since it is possible God prefers the same amicable settlement for a wife's 'nushuz' to beating her. Perhaps this was the thinking of Imam Shafi (n.d.) when he remarked, "It is preferable not to resort to the chastisement of the wife."

Let us now examine the relevant section of 2:228 that is applicable to the respective positions of husband and wife. The two parts of this section of 2:228 are interrelated and need to be considered jointly as well as separately. This section of 2:228 says, " . . . and women shall have rights similar to the rights against them, according to what is equitable; but men have a degree (of advantage) over them." The latter part of this section of 2:228 which says, "but men have a degree (of advantage) over them" has been a point of great controversy among Islamic theologians and Islamic jurists. However, this part of the relevant section of 2:228 must not be read in isolation or considered out of context. A careful analysis of verse 2:228 shows this special advantage of men over women relates clearly to women who are divorced by their husbands through *talaq*. This verse deals with the waiting period after *talaq* and other details about divorced women (*al-mutallaqaatu*) divorced through *talaq*. The full text of 2:228 says the following:

"Divorced women (*al-mutallaqaatu*) shall wait concerning themselves for three monthly periods. Nor is it lawful for them to hide what God has created in their wombs, if they have faith in God and the Last Day. And their husbands have the better right to take them back in that period, if they wish for reconciliation. And women shall have rights similar to the rights against them, according to what is equitable; but men have a degree (of advantage) over them. And God is Exalted in Power, Wise."

It is noticeable that except for the last part of 2:228 which says, "men have a degree (of advantage) over them" the focus of this verse is on the absolute equality of men and women in the matter of divorce by *talaq*. The last part of 2:228, which mentions the degree of advantage enjoyed by men over women, clearly refers to the sole right of men to divorce their wives through *talaq* which is denied to wives who must use other procedures of divorce such as *khula, mubaraa,* and court proceedings. Having considered this solitary area of a husband's superiority over a woman in *talaq* divorce, we are left with the major part of 2:228 which treats men and women with complete equality particularly when it says, " . . . *wa lahunna mislullazii alaihinna bil maaruf*" which means " . . . and women shall have rights similar to the rights against them, according to what is equitable." Commenting on this section of 2:228, Maulana Abul Kalam Azad (1980) opines that these words of the Quran revolutionized the life of mankind by its declaration of equal rights of men and women in Muslim society. Analyzing the concept of '*maaruf*,' Lane (1980) opines that being a passive article of the verbal root 'to know,' '*maaruf*' indicates obviously or conveniently accepted or well-known things. With regard to treatment that is '*maaruf*,' Milton Cowan (1976) thinks that the expression '*maaruf*' has dimensions of equitable, courteous, and beneficial. It is therefore clear from the above discussion that Islamic principles laid down by the Quran accept the equitable and equal treatment of men and women.

The expression *'darajat'* is mentioned in the Quran in the following verses.

- "It is He who has made you (His) agents, inheritors of the earth: He has raised you in ranks, some above others (*wa rafaa bazakum fawqa baazin darajaatin*)." (6:165)

- "It is We who portion out between them their livelihood in the life of this world: and We raise some of them above others in rank (*wa rafanaa bazahum fawqabazin darajaatin*) so that some may command work from others." (43:32)

In both these verses of the Quran no specific preference is given to men over women but preference is given to some over others irrespective of their sexes. Again, the equality of the husband and the wife is emphasized in 2:187 of the Quran says, "They (your wives) are your garments and you (the husbands) are their (your wives) garments . . . " Thus, 2:187 tells us God has given the husband and the wife a complimentary role to each other neither one dominating the other. In view of the above discussion, it is clear the Quran and the Hadith created a revolution in Arab society with regard to the respective position of husband and wife in the seventh century A.D. It is unfortunate that Islamic teachings on this subject continue to be ignored by Muslim societies. It is hoped the real messages of the Quran and the Hadith will be looked at again and acted upon in our time.

7

Rules of Dissolution
of Marriage in Islamic Law

Although divorce is permitted in Islamic law, it is discouraged by both the Quran and the Hadith. The Prophet (pbuh) said, "With Allah the most detestable of all things permitted is divorce". (AD 13:3) The Quran recommends reconciliation between the couple before a breach between the husband and wife (*shiqaq baynakum*) leads to divorce. Quranic verses relevant for this subject are given below.

- "If you fear a breach between them twain, appoint (two) arbiters, one from his family, and the other from hers; If they wish for peace, God will cause their reconciliation: For God has full knowledge, and is acquainted with all things." (4:35)

- "And if a wife fears cruelty or desertion on her husband's part, there is no blame on them if they arrange an amicable settlement between themselves; and such settlement is best; even though men's souls are swayed by greed. But if you do good and practise selfrestraint, God is well acquainted with all that you do." (4:128)

- "But if they disagree (and must part) God will provide abundance for all from His all-reaching bounty; For God is He that cares for all and is Wise." (4:130)

- "Divorced women shall wait concerning themselves for three monthly periods. Nor is it lawful for them to hide what God has created in their wombs, if they have faith in God and the Last

59

Day. And their husbands have the better right to take them back in that period, if they wish for reconciliation; and women shall have rights similar to the rights against them according to what is equitable . . . "(2:228)

- "A divorce is only permissible twice: after that parties should either hold together on equitable terms or separate with kindness. It is not lawful for you (men) to take back (from your wives) any of your gifts, except when both parties fear that they would be unable to keep the limits ordained by God. If you (judges) do indeed fear that they would be unable to keep the limits ordained by God, there is no blame on either of them if she gives something for her freedom. These are the limits ordained by God; so do not transgress them. If any do transgress the limits ordained by God, such persons wrong (themselves as well as others)." (2:229)

- "So if a husband divorces his wife (irrevocably), he cannot, after that, remarry her until after she has married another husband and he has divorced her. In that case there is no blame on either of them if they reunite, provided they feel that they can keep the limits ordained by God. . . . " (2:230)

- "When you divorce women, and they fulfil the term of their (iddat), either take them back on equitable terms or set them free on equitable terms; but do not take them back to injure them, (or) to take undue advantage. If anyone does that, he wrongs his own soul . . . " (2:231)

- "When you divorce women, and they fulfil the term of their (iddat), do not prevent them from marrying their (former) husbands, if they mutually agree on equitable terms. This instruction is for all amongst you, who believes in God and the Last Day . . . " (2:232)

- "There is no blame on you if you divorce women before consummation or the fixation of their Dower; but bestow on them (a suitable gift), the wealthy according to his means, and the poor according to his means—a gift of a reasonable amount is due from those who wish to do the right thing.

  And if you divorce them before consummation, but after the fixation of a Dower for them, then the half of the Dower (is due to them), unless they remit it or (the man's half) is remitted by him in whose hands is the marriage tie; and the remission (of the man's half) is the nearest to righteousness and do not forget liberality between yourselves. For God sees well all that you do." (2:236–237)

- "O Prophet! When you divorce women, divorce them at their prescribed periods, and count (accurately) their prescribed periods: and fear God your Lord: and turn them not out of their houses, nor shall they (themselves) leave, except in case they are guilty of some open lewdness, those are limits set by God: and any who transgresses the limits of God, does verily wrong his (own) soul . . . " (65:1)

- "Thus when they fulfil their term appointed, either take them back on equitable terms or part with them on equitable terms; and take for witness two persons from among you, endowed with justice, and establish the evidence (as) before God . . . " (65:2)

- "Such of your women as have passed the age of monthly courses, for them the prescribed period, if you have any doubts, is three months, and for those who have no courses (it is the same): for those who carry (life within their wombs), their period is until they deliver their burdens: and for those who fear God, He will make their path easy." (65:4)

- "Let the women live (in iddat) in the same style as you live, according to your means: annoy them not, so as to restrict them. And if they carry (life in their wombs), then spend (your substance) on them until they deliver their burden: and if they suckle your (offspring), give them their recompense: and take mutual counsel together, according to what is just and reasonable. And if you find yourselves in difficulties, let another woman suckle (the child) on the (father's) behalf.

  Let the man of means spend according to his means: and the man whose resources are restricted, let him spend according to what God has given him. God puts no burden on any person beyond what He has given him. After a difficulty, God will soon grant relief." (65:6–7)

- "For divorced women maintenance (should be provided) on a reasonable (scale). This, is a duty on the righteous." (2:241)

- "But if you decide to take one wife in place of another, even if you had given the latter a whole treasure for Dower, take not the least bit of it back; would you take it by slander and a manifest wrong?

  And how could you take it when you have gone in unto each other, and they have taken form you a solemn covenant?" (4:20–21)

- "O you who believe! When you marry believing women, and then divorce them before you have touched them, no period of iddat have you to count in respect of them: so give them a present, and set them free in a handsome manner." (33:49)

- "Those of you who die and leave widows should bequeath for their widows a year's maintenance and residence; but if they leave (the residence), there is no blame on you for what they do with themselves, provided it is reasonable. And God is Exalted in Power, Wise." (2:240)

- "And give the woman (on marriage) their Dower as a free gift; but if they, of their own good pleasure, remit any part of it to you, take it and enjoy it with right good cheer." (4:4)

The verses of the Quran quoted above relate to the various aspects of *talaq* divorce, *iddat*, *dower*, and maintenance. Verses 4:35, 4:128, 2:228, and 2:231 deal with arbitration regarding *talaq* divorce, reconciliation among couples, and divorcing and freeing the wife by the husband on equitable terms. Verses 2:229, 2:236, 2:237, 4:4, 4:20–21, 33:49, 65:6, and 65:7 deal with dower and suitable gifts and presents to be given to the divorced wife by the husband. Verses 2:229 and 2:230 address the situation when *talaq* is irrevocable. Verse 2:229 also deals with the wife giving something to her husband for her release from the matrimonial tie. The wife's right to divorce her husband through the *khula* procedure is based on 2:229. Verse 2:232 deals with the right of the divorced wife to marry a different person other than the divorcer after the irrevocable *talaq*. Verse 2:230 deals with the procedure for re-marrying the divorced wife after the irrevocable *talaq*. Verses 2:228, 33:49, 65:1, and 65:4 deal with *iddat* or the prescribed period of waiting to be completed by the divorced wife. Verse 2:241 deals with the maintenance of the divorced woman by the divorcing husband. Verse 65:6 addresses the maintenance of the divorced wife by the divorcing husband until the termination of pregnancy, if any, and until the child is weaned. Verse 2:240 deals with the maintenance of a widow by the deceased husband's estate (for a limited period in particular circumstances) through the provisions in a will.

THE HUSBAND'S RIGHT OF DIVORCE (*TALAQ*)

Talaq (or divorce by husband) literally means freeing or undoing of a knot (Raghib 1485). This is one of the three modes of dissolution of marriage in Islam, the other two being divorce by the wife in special circumstances and divorce by judicial decree. Although divorce by *talaq* is the exclusive right of the husband, it has limitations. Thus, despite being an extrajudicial proceeding, the role of the arbiter in the *talaq* mode of divorce makes *talaq* a quasijudicial proceeding. Verse 4:35 of the Quran specifically asks for the appointment of two arbiters (one each for the husband and the wife) to effect reconciliation among them when a breach between the two is apprehended. It is in keeping with the dictates of the Quran if the *talaq* of the wife by the husband is accepted as effective, provided the tribunal representing each party come to the decision that the *talaq* is effective. The Muslim Family Law Ordinance 1961 of Pakistan and Bangladesh followed exactly the recommendation of 4:35 regarding arbiters to give effect to a *talaq*. In addition to the limitation of 4:35, the rules of *iddat* prescribed by the Quran in the verses 2:228, 33:49, 65:1, and 65:4 must be observed by the wife when she is divorced by her husband. The divorce becomes irrevocable only after the conditions of 2:229 and 2:230 are fulfilled. Since intercourse is prohibited among married couples when the wife's course (*quru*) is on (2:222), the Prophet (pbuh) did not allow Ibne Umar to divorce his wife during her course (BU 68:1). Therefore, *talaq* is only permitted in the state of *tuhr* (when the wife is clear from menstrual discharge) and intercourse between couples during *tuhr*, is not permitted.

Despite the clear wordings of 2:228 and 2:229 regarding *iddat* (the three month waiting period), the permissibility of *talaq* only twice, and the right of the husband to take the divorced wife back during that period, a peculiar innovation surreptitiously crept into Islamic rules of divorce in the shape of '*talaq ul bid'i*' or "triple *talaq*." Since that time, jurists of Islamic law recognize three forms of *talaq*, namely, *talaq ahsan*, *talaq hasan*, and *talaq bid'i*.

Talaq ahsan (the best method of *talaq*) is the only form of *talaq* recognized by the Quran. *Talaq ahsan* occurs when the *talaq* is pronounced by the husband in a *tuhr* (when a woman is clear from her menstrual discharge) only once, and then is followed by *iddat* (period of waiting) (al-Marghinani 1982). During the period of *iddat*, the husband has the right to revoke the *talaq*. This mode of *talaq* is also called *talaq al-sunna* as it was approved by the Prophet Muhammad (pbuh).

Talaq hasan (the good method of *talaq*) is a mode of *talaq* in which the husband divorces his wife for the first time in one *tuhr*, followed by a second divorce in the second *tuhr* and followed again by a third divorce in the third *tuhr*. In this way, he divorces his wife thrice in one *iddat*.

"Talaq bid'i or *talaqi thalatha fi majlisin wahidin"* (triple divorce in one sitting) is an innovation of *talaq* introduced after the death of the Prophet Muhammad (pbuh). According to this form of *talaq,* a man would pronounce *talaq* (divorce) three times in one sitting and this would be understood as if *talaq* (divorce) had been given thrice. This is the most widely practiced form of *talaq* among Muslims, particularly in India, Pakistan, and Bangladesh. This mode of *talaq* has raised tremendous controversy between the supporters and opposers of triple *talaq.* The supporters of *talaq bid'i* argue that the Quran has not laid any specific method of *talaq* and the Prophet (pbuh) never indicated that *talaq bid'i* would not be valid. Imam Ibne Hazam (d. 456 AH) gave a detailed argument in favor of triple *talaq* in one sitting. Hazam relies on some interpretations of Quranic verses that favor *talaq bid'i* and also quote some alleged Hadith in favor of triple *talaq.* However, no Quranic verse has ever supported the triple *talaq* in one sitting. A thorough study of the history of Islam, Quranic verses, and authentic Hadith, lead to the inevitable conclusion that triple *talaq* in one sitting cannot be considered irrevocable divorce under Islamic rules. The following points lead to this conclusion:

- There is no mention of the triple *talaq* in one sitting in the Quran or in the Hadith.

- There is no mention in the history of Islam about the practice of triple *talaq* in one sitting during the time of the Prophet (pbuh). According to Nesai (one of the collectors of the six Sahihs), the Prophet (pbuh) became extremely angry when he was told of a Muslim who had divorced his wife thrice in one sitting and the Prophet (pbuh) said: "You make fun of Allah's Book and I am still there among you" (al-Asqalani 1982). This Hadith does not say the Prophet (pbuh) accepted a triple *talaq* in one sitting while condemning such a method.

- There was no practice of triple divorce in one sitting during the Caliphate of Abu Bakr.

- Umar I enforced triple *talaq* in one sitting in the latter period of his Caliphate (al-Asqalani 1982). During the first two years of the Caliphate of Umar I a pronouncement of triple divorce in one sitting was considered as *talaq-i-raj'i* (revocable divorce).

- Even after Umar I's introduction of *talaq bid'i* Caliph Ali insisted on the provision of arbitration under 4:35. This is what he told a husband who did not fulfill the condition of verse 4:35 (Razi n.d.).

- Many eminent *ashabs* of the Prophet (pbuh), such as Abdullah bin Masud, Abdur Rahman Bin Awf, and Zubayr Bin al-Awam maintained that triple *talaq* in one sitting should not be considered *talaq-i-battah* (irrevocable divorce).

The above position changed when the four schools of Sunni law were established. Even among these four Sunni schools of law, the triple *talaq* in one sitting received reluctant acceptance. Imam Abu Hanifah and Imam Malik Bin Anas considered triple *talaq* in one sitting as *bidah* and not permissible. Strangely enough, both Imam Abu Hanifah and Imam Malik held the view that although not permissible, once pronounced thrice, the triple *talaq* in one sitting would be a valid *talaq* and an effective and irrevocable *talaq* (*talaq-i-battah*). Although considering triple *talaq* in one sitting as *bidah* in the beginning of his career, Imam Ahmed Bin Hanbal considered triple *talaq* in one sitting as *talaq-i-battah*. However, despite his earlier view, Imam Hanbal revised his opinion later and observed there was no mention of triple divorce in one sitting in the Quran and such a divorce was *talaq-i-raj'i* (revocable divorce), and therefore has no legal validity. A fourteenth century A.D. Hanbali jurist, Imam Ibne Taymiyah (n.d.) declared in his *fatwa* (legal opinion) that such was the view of Imam Ahmed Ibne Hanbal and that the triple *talaq* in one sitting would have no legal validity. Ibne Qayyim, a disciple of Ibne Taymiyah, held that triple *talaq* in one sitting would result in only one revocable divorce and, in support of his view, mentioned the historical fact that not even twenty of the disciples (*ashabs*) of the Prophet's (pbuh) 100,000 disciples (*ashabs*) ever agreed on the validity of the triple *talaq* in one sitting (Rahman 1985). Among the four founders of the four Sunni schools of law, Imam Shafii (n.d.) was the only one who considered triple divorce in one sitting as permissible and sanctioned by the Quran. Among modern Islamic jurists, Maulana Maudoodi (1987) tried to justify the validity of the triple *talaq* in one sitting on the basis of a very weak Hadith. According to this inauthentic Hadith, the Prophet (pbuh) is alleged to have declared in a conversation with Abdullah Ibne Umar that the triple *talaq* pronounced in one sitting, although sinful, was irrevocable. It is difficult to accept that the Prophet (pbuh) would give binding force to an act that he considered sinful. The expression, "*Al-talaqu marratan*" (divorce may be pronounced twice), in 2:229 of the Quran, has been advanced as an argument against the validity of the triple divorce in one sitting by Maulana Umar Ahmed Usmani (1980). According to Usmani, the word '*marratan*' clearly shows there must be a time gap between the two divorces, the *talaq* divorce cannot be pronounced twice at the same sitting, and the *talaq* can be pronounced by the husband only once at a time.

The Egyptian journalist and renowned Islamic scholar, Muhammad Hussain Haykal, attempted to justify Caliph Umar I's decision sanctioning the three *talaqs* in one sitting as irrevocable. According to Haykal, Caliph Umar I introduced this innovation in order to accommodate the demands of newly captured women from Syria and Egypt on their prospective Arab husbands to divorce their former wives in one sitting. (Engineer 1992). Undoubtedly, this is a weak justification for an innovation clearly opposed to 2:228 and 2:229 of the Quran and one that has no support from authentic Hadiths. Therefore, such a divorce is clearly un-Islamic. The weakness of Umar I's order enforcing triple *talaq* in one sitting can be further shown when one considers the effects of 4:35 and 65:2. According to 4:35, the husband's right of divorce is not unconditional as the enforcement of the husband's *talaq* divorce must be preceded by arbitration between the husband and the wife. On the basis of 4:35 Caliph Ali gave a ruling that the decision of arbiters should be binding (Engineer 1992). From this discussion, as well as following 4:35, we can safely conclude that in the matter of *talaq* divorce the *qadi* or the court should be the final authority. On careful consideration of 65:2 of the Quran, which asks husbands to take their wives back on equitable terms or part with them on equitable terms, it appears the pronouncement of triple divorce in one sitting by a husband in anger is clearly against this verse. In view of the above that despite the opinions of many jurists of the four Sunni schools of law and that of Caliph Umar I favoring the irrevocability of the triple *talaq* in one sitting, we cannot accept this mode of *talaq* as an approved Islamic mode of divorce.

THE WIFE'S RIGHT OF DIVORCE

Talaq divorce by wife

The Quran makes no reference about women pronouncing *talaq* on their husbands, but at the same time there is no indication in the Quran that the woman's right of repudiating her husband by divorce, prevailing in pre-Islamic Arabia was removed by Islamic laws. It can be argued that as the Quran prescribes mutual and peaceful reconciliation or separation on peaceful terms after the decision of the arbiter, the wife also has the right of repudiating her husband.

Khula and *Mubaraa*

The wife's right to claim divorce is recognized by the Quran and by the Hadith and is accepted by the jurists of Islamic law. It can have either of the two forms, namely '*khula*' and '*mubaraa*'. If the desire to separate comes from the wife, it is called *khula* or *khul*. If the divorce is the result of mutual aversion (and consent) it is called *mubaraa*.

The word '*khul*,' popularly known as '*khula*,' '*khoola*' or '*khala*' literally means "to take off clothes and then to lay down one's authority over a wife." According to Fyzee (1964) a wife can propose a *khula* divorce of her husband in which she is released (from marriage) by her husband and agrees to give a consideration (*iwad* or return) to her husband for her release from the marriage. This consideration is a matter of arrangement between the parties and as a consideration for this bargain the wife may return the dower (mahr) or release her husband from paying the outstanding dower. This rule (of the wife giving consideration to the husband for her release from the marriage) can be extended in modern times in the shape of the wife giving other rights to the husband or returning other benefits for the benefit of the husband. The wife's right of *khula* divorce is based on 2:229 of the Quran and two Hadiths in Bukhari's collection of Hadith. The first of these two Hadiths relates to the Prophet (pbuh) personally. According to it the Prophet (pbuh) married Umaima and when he went to her she said that she sought refuge in God from him (i.e. she wanted a divorce) and the Prophet (pbuh) granted her the divorce and sent her off with some presents (B 68:3). The other Hadith tells us Jamilah, the wife of Thabit Ibn Qais, went to the Prophet (pbuh) and said, "O Messenger of Allah! I do not find fault in Thabit Ibn Qais regarding his morals or faith but I cannot pull on with him (a different report said that she said 'I cannot bear with him')." To this the Prophet (pbuh) said, "Will you return to him his orchard (which he had settled upon her as her dower)?" She replied to the Prophet (pbuh), "Certainly O Messenger of Allah and I am prepared to give even more!" Hearing this the Prophet (pbuh) called Thabit and told Jamilah, "No, nothing more, only give him back his orchard." Then the Prophet (pbuh) told Thabit to accept the garden and to agree to divorce Jamilah (B 68:11). Maudoodi (1987) quotes a Hadith narrated by Imam Malik and Abu Daud. According to this Hadith, Habibah, the second wife of Thabit, complained to the Prophet (pbuh) that they (the couple) could no longer get on together and offered all that Thabit had given her in exchange for her release from the marriage. The Prophet (pbuh) asked Thabit to divorce Habibah in exchange for what he had given to her. In *mubaraa* divorce by the wife, both the parties agree to be free from each other and that is why *mubaraa* divorce comes into affect by mutual consent or aversion of both the parties. There are differing opinions on *'iwad'* (consideration) needed for *khula*, or *mubaraa*, divorce by the wife. According to Fyzee (1964), after the dissolution of the marriage by mutual consent is proven, the question of *iwad* (either by the wife giving up her right of *mahr*, or making compensation to the husband), is a matter to be determined in each case. Fyzee further opines there is no presumption the husband has been released of his duty to pay *mahr* to his wife. However, Hanafi authorities differ in their opinions. Imam Abu Hanifa opines that in the absence of agreement of the parties, the dower is deemed to be relinquished by the wife both in *khula* and *mubaraa* forms of divorce. Imam Abu Yusuf (a Hanafi jurist) disagrees with Abu Hanifa and says that the relinquishment of the dower by the wife applies to *mubaraa* divorce and not to *khula* divorce. Imam Muhammad, another Hanafi jurist who disagrees with both Abu Hanifa and Abu Yusuf, holds the view that the dower is not relinquished by the wife in either *khula* or *mubaraa* divorce. In view of the differing opinions among the Hanafis, Fyzee (1964) suggests the courts should be the final authority. However, Muhammad Ali (1950), arguing on the strength of 4:35, came to the conclusion that it was for the arbiter to decide about the entitlement (or otherwise) of the dower by the wife on the basis of whether or not the husband or the wife is responsible for the breach.

Maudoodi (1987) mentions two precedents about *khula* divorce. The first precedent relates to a decision of Caliph Umar I, when he granted *khula* divorce to an adamant wife (who refused to patch things up despite his counsel and three days of confinement), and he said to the husband, "Grant her separation (divorce), even if it be in return for her earrings." The second precendent relates to a decision of Caliph Usman regarding Rukayyah Binte Muawwiz whose plea for divorcing her husband was accepted by the Caliph (despite the husband's refusal to divorce) in exchange for all the properties of Rukayyah, which she offered to her husband for getting the divorce. From the above two precedents, and the Prophet's (pbuh) decision about Thabit's wives Maudoodi (1987) deduces the following seven rules for *khula* divorce:

- *Khula* divorce will be enforced only if the wife has a deep dislike for her husband and refuses to live with her husband. In essence this is equivalent to the western concept of incompatibility.

- The two requirements of the wife's hatred and dislike for her husband and the impossibility of the couples continuing their marriage tie must be proved beyond reasonable doubt to the judge granting *khula* divorce.

- Once these two requirements for granting *khula* divorce are proven, the judge need not go into the causes of these two requirements.

- While the judge has the right to counsel the wife to withdraw her claim for *khula* divorce, the judge has no right to force the wife to continue with the marriage against her will.

- The judge need not find out whether a wife's request for *khula* divorce is based on genuine need or whether it is the result of her sexual desire.

- The *khula* divorce has all the effects of *talaq-i-battah* (irrevocable divorce).

- In the absence of any limit to the amount of consideration for *khula* in the Quran, it is up to the spouses to agree upon the amount.

It appears that Maudoodi's seventh rule for *khula* divorce is incorrect as the Prophet (pbuh) is reported to have said that the man agreeing to *khula* divorce to his wife should not take from his wife more than what he gave her. Caliph Ali also declared that it was undesirable for the *iwad* (consideration) for *khula* to be more than the dower and most Sunni jurists agree with this view.

Despite the Islamic right of *khula* and *mubaraa* given to the wife by the aforesaid authorities, the courts of law in the Indian subcontinent were reluctant to grant this fundamental right to women. In the case of Sayeeda Khanam versus Muhammad Sahi (PLD 1952 Lahore 113), a full bench of the Lahore High Court held that the wife cannot claim divorce (*khula*) on grounds of incompatibility of temperament, dislike, or even hatred for the husband. The only course open to her is to persuade her husband to release her from the marriage. The court held that: "If the wives were allowed to dissolve their marriage without the consent of their husbands by merely giving up their Dowers, paid or promised to be paid, the institution of marriage would be meaningless as there would be no stability attached to it." Without a doubt this particular judgment is against the principle laid down by 2:229 of the Quran. However, this decision was changed by the Supreme Court of Pakistan. In the case of Khurshid Bibi versus Mohammad Amin (PLD 1967 Supreme Court 97), the Supreme Court of Pakistan held there are two classes of cases of *khula*, by mutual agreement and by order of the *qazi* or court. In the first category of *khula* the husband dissolves the marriage by pronouncing a *talaq*, the sanction for such a *khula* is found in reasoning and deduction from 2:229 or from the contract of the two parties to the marriage contract. Sanctions for *khula* under an order of the *qazi* (court) is found in the express words of 2:229. This decision of the Supreme Court of Pakistan is the current law for *khula* in Pakistan and Bangladesh. The courts of India also accepted *khula* as a mode of dissolution of a Muslim marriage in 1968. The case of Ghansi Bibi versus Ghulam Dastagir (AIR 1968 I Mysore 566) held that, "A Muslim marriage may be dissolved by pronouncing *talaq*. It may also be dissolved by an agreement between the husband and wife. When it is the latter, it is known as *khula*."

Among Muslim jurists, some consider *khula* a divorce and others consider it a *faskh* (annulment of marriage). Those who consider *khula* a divorce, support their view by saying the husband has to pronounce the divorce after the wife returns the dower (in full or in part). Those who consider *khula* as *faskh* support their view in that *khula* terminates the marriage without the husband pronouncing the divorce. Actually, it does not matter if *khula* is a *talaq* or *faskh* as in both of these cases it comes under the category of divorce as understood in the Western world.

An interesting point is made by Mulla (n.d.) on the consequences of *khula* and *mubaraa* divorce on maintenance after such a divorce. Mulla opines that unless a contrary term is included in the contract, *khula* or *mubaraa* divorce operates as a release by the wife of her dower, but the husband's liability of maintaining the wife during her *iddat* is not affected nor does it affect the husband's duty to maintain his children by her.

Talaq-I-Tafwid (delegated divorce)

This right of divorce can be exercised by the wife if it was given to the wife by the husband at the time of the marriage. Sir Abdur Rahim (n.d.) summarizes the rules of *talaq-i-tafwid* in *Principles of Mohammadan Jurisprudence*. Rahim tells us that the delegation of the power of divorce by the husband to the wife is usually done at the time of the marriage and through the terms of the '*nikah namah*' (marriage contract). Such a conferring of the right of divorce to the wife is called *tafwid*, or delegation. Once the power is delegated to the wife, the husband cannot revoke it. It is up to the wife to exercise or not to exercise this power. The delegation (*tafwid*) of this power may be in three forms. They are: (1) *al-ikhtiar* (the choice) when the husband delegates the power of divorce by saying, choose thyself or divorce thyself (2) *al-amru bil yadi* (the act is in your hand) when the husband delegates the power of divorce to his wife by saying, 'your business is your business' (3) *al-mashiat* when the husband delegates this power of divorce by saying, 'if you wish, divorce yourself.'

In Pakistan and India the courts have expanded the rules of *talaq-i-tafwid*. Thus, the delegation of this power must be expressly made, not implied (Sayeeda Khanam vs. Muhammad Sahi PLD 1952 Lahore 89). The pronouncement of *talaq* by the wife need not be in the presence of the husband or witness and the delegated power of divorce for nonpayment of dower is not valid (Tahazzad Hossain Sikdar vs. Hossneara Begum (PLD 1967 Dacca 421). The delegation of the right of divorce can be conditional or unconditional (Aklima Khatun vs. Mohibur Rahman and others PLD 1963 Dacca 602). This delegation of the power of divorce would not deprive the husband of his own right to divorce his wife under certain circumstances (Rahman 1985). The following conditions were held to be valid, reasonable, and binding on the parties if *talaq-i-tafwid* is delegated to the wife and *talaq-i-tafwid* can take place if such conditions are violated. The conditions, based on legal precedents throughout the Indian subcontinent, are as follows:

- The husband should earn his livelihood and should live a respectable life. He should maintain his wife and should live in a house approved by her.

- The husband should not beat or ill-treat his wife.

- If the husband oppresses his wife wrongfully she will be entitled to reside at her father's house and to get maintenance from him.

- The husband should allow his wife to be taken to her father's house four times a year.

- If the wife be in need of going to and coming back from her father's residence, he would send her there and bring her back at his own expense.

- The husband would not contract a second marriage without the consent of his wife.

- The husband would contract a second marriage only if she is either barren or perpetually ill.

- The husband should pay his wife dower on demand.

- The husband would not take any remission of dower from the wife except in the presence of her relations.

MAFQUD-AL-KHABAR (DIVORCE OF A MISSING HUSBAND)

Both the Quran and the Hadith are silent regarding the waiting period of a wife if the husband is missing and cannot be communicated with. In view of the absence of any authority from the Quran or from the Hadith, a reasonable period of waiting should be sufficient for the wife to be free from the marriage with such a person. However, the Hanafi jurists took a very unreasonable and oppressive view on this question. Thus Imam Abu Hanifa opined that women in such cases should wait for 120 years. Imam Yusuf asked for an unreasonably long waiting period of 100 years for women in this position. Imam Shafii recommended seven years waiting for wives of the *mafqud-al-khabar*. However, other jurists approached this issue more reasonably. Imam Malik recommended four years in such cases. Ibn Musayyal opined, "When a person becomes *mufqud* in the course of fighting, his wife shall wait for a year." However, no Hadith was quoted on this subject but this statement is quoted by Bukhari in his collection in the chapter of *mafqud* (B 68:21). In an attempt to reform the laws of the dissolution of Muslim marriages, the British authority in India, enacted the Dissolution of Muslim Marriage Act 1939. On this subject, the 1939 Act adopted the Maliki view. Thus, under Section 2(1) of the Dissolution of Muslim Marriage Act 1939, a Muslim wife is entitled to divorce her husband on the grounds that the whereabouts of her husband have not been known for a period of four years. Since the Quran and the Hadith are silent on this subject, it is reasonable to state the Maliki view as well as section 2(1) of the 1939 Act conform with the principles of Islam.

THE ROLE OF COURTS OF LAW AND ARBITRATORS

The courts of law as we find in modern times were not in existence when the Prophet Muhammad (pbuh) started his mission in 610 A.D. The Prophet (pbuh) himself was simultaneously head of state and head of the judiciary of the Muslim state of Medina from 622 A.D. to 632 A.D. The rudimentary judicial system of Islam, starting with the appointment of Muadh Bin Jabal as the leader and the 'qadi' of the Muslim immigrants going to Yemen, developed slowly during the Caliphate of the first four Caliphs. However, the judiciary did not take definite shape until the development of the four Sunni Schools of Islamic law in the middle of the fourth century AH. Similar developments took place among the Shiahs who formed their own Shariah and legal system. Various verses of the Quran and collections of the Prophet's (pbuh) Hadiths took the most prominent part in the development of the judicial systems among Muslims. The Shariah, however, allowed the growth of parallel rules of actions for Muslims in both legal (as we understand today) and nonlegal matters. The institution of marriage and divorce in Islam had both religious and legal character. Therefore, on the question of the dissolution of Muslim marriage, decisions were taken from both inside and outside the courts. While unilateral action by the husband in the matter of *talaq* divorce and bilateral actions by both spouses in the matter of *khula* and *mubaraa* dissolution of marriages were approved, there was always some control over such actions by the state and/or the judiciary of the Muslim state. Through verse 4:35, the Quran itself gives clear approval to judicial or quasi-judicial intervention in the dissolution of Muslim marriage when it said, "If you fear breach between them twain, appoint (two) arbiters, one from his family, and the other from her..." (4:35). Caliph Ali enforced the decision of an arbiter in separating a married couple. By the time the four Sunni schools of law took a definite shape, various Sunni schools of law had developed roles for the intervention of the courts in matters of judicial dissolution or annulments of Muslim marriages. The Hanafi jurists however, gave wives very restricted rights to terminate their marriages with the help of the courts. Thus Hanafi law allowed only annulment of the marriage and the declaration of the termination of the marriage between a woman and her missing husband. A Hanafi woman could apply to the court for the annulment of her marriage on the grounds that her husband proved unable to consummate the marriage (provided his sexual impotence was unknown to the wife at the time of the marriage contract), or she could apply to the court for a declaration that her marriage with her missing husband be terminated through his presumed death. However, this second right of a Hanafi woman is of very limited value due to the unusually long waiting period. The Shafi, Hanbali, and Maliki schools of law conferred valuable rights on Muslim women to dissolve their marriages through the courts on the grounds of the husband's failure to fulfill his marital duties. Thus, according to these schools of law, the court played a role when the husband failed to maintain his wife, when the husband was impotent, or when the husband was disabled. Let us take a closer look at these circumstances and the provisions made by the various schools of law.

The first situation to consider is when a husband has the ability to maintain his wife but does not do so. The Hanafi law gives no help to the wife who does not receive any maintenance from her husband even if he can afford to pay. In such cases, Hanafi jurists ask the woman to find ways to meet her living expenses. The Maliki law, however, allows the court to separate spouses in such cases by pronouncing a decree of divorce. Some Hanafi jurists approve of this Maliki law provided either the woman is incapable of maintaining herself or she faces the danger of overstepping the limits of Allah. Maudoodi (1987) rejects the Hanafi provision. According to Maudoodi, the Quran grants the wife living expenses from her husband because the husband is responsible for his wife's maintenance as long as the marriage lasts. Verses 65:6 and 65:7 support the view of Maudoodi in this matter.

Another situation arises when the husband cannot afford to pay maintenance to his wife. Here again, Hanafi law is against the court's intervention to help a wife who has been deprived of her husband's maintenance. In such cases, Hanafi jurists urge the women to face the situation with patience or to borrow or seek help from her relatives. Imam Abu Hanifa justifies this unsympathetic Hanafi ruling by reasoning that maintenance of the wife in such cases is the responsibility of the person who would have maintained her if she were not married. Imam Malik, Imam Shafii, and Imam Hanbal all agree the court has the right to intervene and separate the spouses if a woman cannot resolve the issue with her husband and asks the court for a separation. While Imam Hanbal supports immediate separation in such cases, Imam Malik recommends one or two months notice to the husband before the separation but Imam Shafii thinks three days notice is enough (Maudoodi 1987). The opinions of Imam Malik, Imam Shafii, and Imam Ahmed bin Hanbal are supported by the Quranic verses that grant conjugal rights to the husband in return for money he spends for his wife. The opinions of these three Imams are also supported by a Hadith (quoted by Darqutni and Baihaqi), which says in cases of nonpayment of living expenses, the spouses should be separated. This ruling of the three Imams also has support from the rulings of Caliph Umar, Caliph Ali, Caliph Umar II, and those of Abu Huraira and Saad bin Musaal. From the above discussion, it is quite clear the Hanafi ruling on this question is unacceptable and the views of the three other founders of Sunni law are preferable. Following the principle of *takhayyar* (permitting a choice between the conflicting doctrines of various Sunni schools of law), and supported by the Quran, the Hadith, and the decisions of Umar I, Ali, Umar II and of Sahabas, a Hanafi has every right to prefer the views of other Sunni schools in preference to the unacceptable Hanafi view.

There are no rulings of the Quran or the Hadith on the right of divorce if the husband is impotent. Caliph Umar I ruled that separation of the spouses should be made on the grounds of a husband's impotence provided the wife demands it and also provided the husband is still impotent after a year's treatment. However, jurists of the Shariah lay down three unreasonable conditions for such a separation, namely, the woman was unaware of her husband's impotence at the time of marriage; she did not consent to the continuation of her union with her husband after discovering her husband's impotence; and her husband did not have one single intercourse with her. Maudoodi (1987) criticizes these three unreasonable conditions laid down by conservative jurists. Besides, the principles of Islamic fair play, justice, and reason stand against these unreasonable and unauthorized conditions.

Another situation jurists of Islamic law consider is the serious disability of one of the spouses. The Quran does not give any clear or direct guidelines on this matter. However, since the most important objectives of the marital relationship, according to the Quran, are the preservation of chastity, the bond of love and compassion between the spouses, and the avoidance of sources of any harm to the spouses, it is necessary that serious disabilities should give spouses the option to dissolve the marriage (Maudoodi 1987). There are differences of opinion among Sunni jurists on the rights of spouses to dissolve a Muslim marriage on account of the handicap(s) of the other spouse. In his book *Al-Qawanin*, Abu Ejayz (n.d.) listed these handicaps. They include insanity, leprosy, leukoderma, venereal disease, and a foul smelling mouth. According to Abu Ejayz and Imam Malik, a spouse has the right of dissolving the marriage due to any of these handicaps although the spouse has the option of not exercising his or her right and of living with the handicapped spouse. Imam Shafii gives the right to both the spouses of dissolving a marriage if the other spouse is disabled through insanity, leprosy, or leukoderma, but he gives no right to a spouse to dissolve the marriage due to venereal disease, itching, and a foul smelling mouth. Hanafis in general do not confer, on either the husband or the wife, the right of dissolving the marriage on account of any of the aforesaid handicaps however serious it may be. Agreeing with the majority opinions of the Hanafi jurists, Imam Muhammad gives no right to a husband to dissolve the marriage on account of a wife's handicap caused by any of the aforesaid diseases. However, Imam Muhammad supports a wife's right to dissolve the marriage on account of her husband's insanity, leprosy, or leukoderma. Maudoodi (1987) prefers the views of the Malikis and the Shafiis to that of the Hanafis.

Regarding the insanity of the husband, Caliph Umar I ruled that a wife would have the right to be separated from her husband provided the husband's insanity still continues after treatment for one year. However conservative Islamic jurists imposed three unreasonable provisions on this ruling of Caliph Umar I. Imam Abu Hanifa is of the opinion that the ruling of Caliph Umar I is only applicable if the husband was insane before the marriage and was unable to have sexual intercourse after the marriage. Imam Malik fully agrees with the view of Caliph Umar I but other Maliki jurists added three additional conditions. According to conservative jurists, the wife cannot dissolve the marriage: (a) if the husband was insane before the marriage and this fact was known to the wife before the marriage; (b) if after learning about her husband's insanity after marriage the wife continues to live with him; (c) if after learning about her husband's insanity after marriage, the wife allows her husband to have intercourse with her without being compelled. Maudoodi (1987) says these conditions are not supported either by the Quran or the Sunna and are open to serious objections.

From the above discussion on the dissolution of marriages, it is clear Islamic law allows the dissolution of marriage on the petition of either spouse. It is also evident that Islamic law encourages reconciliation in preference to divorce. The Dissolution of Muslim Marriage Act 1939 enacted by the British authority in India is based on Maliki principles and on the fundamentals of Islam relating to marriage and divorce. The courts of law throughout the Muslim world should be given unfettered rights to dissolve marriages on the petition of either spouse. Perhaps then, Muslim women will be granted the rights they were given over 1400 years ago and have been denied to them due to centuries of prejudice.

8

Rights of Custody and Access to Children in Islamic Law

In Islamic law, the technical term for the custody of children is *hizanat*. Elaborate rules have been made by jurists of Islamic law regarding *hizanat*. Unfortunately, there is no direct reference to *hizanat* in the Quran although five Quranic verses, namely 2:233, 31:14, 46:15, and 17:23–24 refer to parents. The first three of these verses refer to the sacrifices and suffering of the mother in bringing up their children. These Quranic verses are given below.

- "The mothers shall give suck to their offspring for two whole years, if the father desires to complete the term. But he shall bear the cost of their food and clothing on equitable terms. No soul shall have a burden laid on it greater than it can bear. No mother shall be treated unfairly on account of her child. Nor father on account of his child..." (2:233)

- "And We have enjoined on man (to be good) to his parents: in travail upon travail did his mother bear him, and in years twain was his weaning; (hear the command), 'Show gratitude to Me and to your parents: to Me is (your final) Goal.'" (31:14)

- "And we have enjoined on man kindness to his parents: in pain did his mother bear him, and in pain did she give him birth. The carrying of (the child) to his weaning is (a period of) thirty months. At length, when he reaches the age of full strength and attains forty years, he says, 'O my Lord! Grant me that I may be grateful for your favour which You have bestowed upon me, and upon both my parents and that I may work righteousness such as You may approve. And be gracious to me in my issue. Truly have I turned to You and truly do I bow (to You) in Islam.'" (46:15)

- "Your Lord has decreed that you worship none but Him, and that you be kind to parents. Whether one or both of them attain old age in your life, say not to them a word of contempt, nor repel them, but address them in terms of honour.

    And, out of kindness, lower to them the wing of humility, and say: 'My Lord! Bestow on them Your Mercy even as they cherished me in childhood.'" (17:23–24)

In explaining 'his weaning within two years' in 31:14, Muhammad Asad (1984) informs us that some philologists think the term *fisal* (weaning) covers the whole period of conception, gestation, birth, and earliest infancy (*tajul arus*) when the child is entirely dependent on its mother. However, the interpretation by most commentators of the Quran, that the period of two years refers to two years after its birth, seems to be more accurate.

While three of the aforesaid verses (2:233, 31:14, 46:15) mention a mother's suffering for her children, none of them give clear guidance about *hizana* (custody of the child). However, the tremendous importance of parents in the life of their children in the early years is asserted by these verses of the Quran and specify the mother's role in carrying, weaning, and giving suck to her child. This had a great effect on the jurists of Islam. This is precisely the reason why, despite being enormously biased in favor of the father in male dominated Muslim society, conservative jurists of Islamic law could not deny the mother's right of custody of very young children. However, the predominately patriarchal atmosphere of this society did not allow them to give custody of the children to the mother after this early stage. In the absence of clear guidance from the Quran, jurists of various schools of Muslim law gave differing decisions on the question of *hizana*.

According to Imam Abu Hanifa, the mother should have the custody of her son until he is capable of eating and dressing himself and can perform his *istinja* (the ritual cleaning of private parts). Allama Khassaf (a Hanafi jurist) opines that custody by the mother ceases at the age of seven years as far as boys are concerned, since a boy that age is capable of performing all the necessary activities for himself without assistance (al-Marghinani 1982). As far as the female child is concerned, the mother, the grandmother, and so forth, have the right of *hizanat* until the first menstruation (the age of puberty). Imam Abu Yusuf has the same view. However, Imam Muhammad thought the mother should have the right of *hizanat* over her daughter until the onset of sexual desire (Rahman 1985). Current Hanafi law gives a mother the custody of a male child until he attains the age of seven years, and of a female child until puberty. Imam Malik is less favorable to the mother. According to Malik, a mother can have custody of a male child until he begins to talk and of the female child until she marries. Among Sunni jurists, Imam Shafii and Imam Hanbal are the most liberal and the most accommodating to women in this matter. According to them, the mother has custody of the child (irrespective of its sex) up to the age of seven and thereafter the child should be given the option to choose between the two parents. The Ithna-Ashari School of law of the Shiahs is the worst in their treatment of the mother. According to the Ithna-Ashari School, the mother has custody of a son up to the age of two and that of a daughter up to the age of seven.

Women's rights of custody (*hizanat*) of their children is further curtailed in the Indian subcontinent (India, Pakistan, and Bangladesh) by disqualifying the mother from having custody under certain circumstances (Baillie 1875). These are: (a) if she marries a man not related to the child within the prohibited degrees of marriage although her disqualification on this ground will end on the dissolution of her second marriage by death or divorce; (b) if she goes to reside at a distance from the child's father's place of residence during the subsistence of her marriage with said father of the child; (c) if she is leading an immoral life (i.e. living as a prostitute or having sex outside marriage); (d) if she neglects to take proper care of the child; (e) if she becomes an apostate.

In the absence of the mother or in the event of her disqualification, *hizana* is given to the father. If the father is unavailable, the right of *hizanat* passes to female relatives in the following order (Hidayatullah 1977) (i) mother's mother, how high so ever (ii) father's mother, how high so ever (iii) full sister, (iv) uterine sister, (v) consanguine sister, (vi) full sister's daughter, (vii) uterine sister's daughter, (viii) consanguine sister's daughter, (ix) maternal aunt in the same order as sisters, (x) paternal aunts in the same order as sisters (Hidayatullah). Neither the consanguine sister nor her daughter is expressly mentioned in *The Hedaya* (al-Marghinani 1982) but Mullah thinks these omissions are accidental. *The Hedaya* justifies a mother's disqualification under circumstance (a) on the grounds that a stepfather who is a stranger would not treat the child with enough kindness. It is noticeable that *The Hedaya* is silent about the father marrying a second wife who is not within the prohibited degree of marriage of the child, although the problem with the stepmother is not rare on the Indian subcontinent. It is because of this stand, of *The Hedaya* and of conservative jurists, that the leading cases on *hizanat* state categorically that the second marriage of the father does not make him unfit to be a guardian (Khatija Begum vs. Ghulam Dastgir AIR 1975 II Andhra 196). In the Indian subcontinent, the father is never disqualified for custody of his child except for apostasy, whereas it is clear the welfare of the child is in jeopardy under the custody or guardianship of a debauched or drunken father. Therefore, the conservative and male dominated Muslim law in the Indian subcontinent awards the custody of a boy over seven years of age and that of an unmarried girl who has attained puberty to the father under any circumstances.

The courts of law in India, Pakistan, and Bangladesh have not always agreed with the conservative Muslim jurists in the matter of *hizanat* and in many cases have awarded *hizanat* to the mother in direct contradiction to Shariah law. In particular, the Lahore High Court took bold steps on various occasions to disentitle the father from custody on account of his conduct (PLD 1953 Lahore 73). The court opined that if the father had been guilty of such conduct that in the opinion of the court should not entitle him to have the custody of the child, then the custody of the child will be denied to him (PLD 1954 Lahore 704). The father's failure to pay maintenance to the children would show that the father was never interested in the welfare of them and therefore would lose his right of *hizanat* over the said minors as such minors should not be deprived of the mother's custody at such a tender age (PLD 1961 Lahore 509). In a case where the mother had brought up the minor child on her own without any financial help from the father, the court refused to give the custody of the minor to the father (PLD 1965 Lahore 695). If not otherwise disqualified, the mother's inability to maintain the child was considered no grounds to deprive her of her right of *hizanat* (PLD 1952 Lahore 73). A mother's poverty was not considered a hindrance to gaining custody of a minor daughter (PLD 1963 Karachi 5). The *hizanat* of an illegitimate child was determined to be always belonging to the mother (AIR 1960 Supreme Court 93). In the Pakistani case of Zohra Begum versus Latif Ahmed Munawar (PLD 1965 Lahore 695) it was decided that, "It would be permissable for courts to differ from the rule of *hizanat* stated in the textbooks of Muslim Law as there is no Quranic or traditional texts on this point. Courts which have taken the place of Qazis can therefore, come to their own conclusions by process of *ijtihad*. It would therefore, be permissible to depart from the rule stated in the textbooks (on *hizanat*) if, on the facts of a given case its application is against the welfare of the minor." In the appeal case of Abu Bakar Siddique (appellant) versus S.M.A. Baker and others (respondent) (DLR 1986 38) the Supreme Court of Bangladesh dealt with the appeal of an application for the custody. In this case their Lordships in the Full Bench dismissed the appeal of the appellant and held that facts point out the welfare of the boy (over seven years of age) requires that his custody should be given to the mother or that she should be appointed as his guardian under Section 25 of the Guardians and Wards Act 1890. In paragraph 23 of their judgment, their Lordships mentioned the welfare provisions of the Guardians and Wards Act 1890 justifying their departure from the traditional Hanafi rule on *hizanat*. This challenge to the traditional Shariah law on *hizanat* by the courts of Pakistan and Bangladesh was neither arbitrary nor baseless as in the absence of clear guidance by the Quran, they based their decisions on many authentic Hadiths dealing with *hizanat*. Some examples follow:

- Baihaqi (n.d.) cites a Hadith wherein the Prophet (pbuh) decided to award *hizanat* of a child to his maternal aunt (right claimed by Jafar, the maternal uncle on behalf of his wife), in preference to the claim of the girl's paternal cousin's daughter, Fatima (right claimed by Fatima through Ali her husband). Thus, the *hizanat* of Hamza's daughter being given to her mother's relation clearly shows the Prophet's (pbuh) preference for the mother.

- Another Hadith quoted by Baihaqi (n.d.) mentions the following incident: "A woman came to the Prophet (pbuh) and said, 'I have a son for whom my womb took the shape of a vessel and my breast looked like a water bag to drink from and my lap was a refuge for him. Now his father has divorced me and wants to take him away from me.' To this the Prophet (pbuh) replied, 'You have a greater right over him (than his father) and therefore you keep him until you remarry.'"

- Another Hadith, quoted in Abu-Daud's collection of Hadiths (n.d.), mentions a mother who had refused to accept Islam but she claimed her right of custody of her daughter over the right of her husband who had embraced Islam. The Prophet (pbuh) made the girl sit between the mother and the father and asked both the parents to call her and said the child would be given to whomever of the two she chose. The girl's initial response was in favor of the mother but finally (guided by Allah in response to the Prophet's (pbuh) prayer) she chose the father.

- Abu Hurairah reports a Hadith that mentions the incident of a woman who came to the Prophet (pbuh) and complained her husband wanted to take away the child from her and the father of the child also came to the Prophet (pbuh). In this case the Prophet (pbuh) addressed the child and told her, "This is your father and this is your mother. Choose my boy anyone you like." The child chose the mother and the Prophet (pbuh) handed him over to her (al-Nesai 1335–37 A.H.).

All these Hadiths clearly show the Prophet's (pbuh) respect for the mother's sentiment as well as for the preference of the child in the matter of *hizanat*. The Pakistani and Bangladeshi judges simply followed these Hadiths. There is also other support for the progressive decisions of these judges. According to Allama Maqdisi (n.d.), "A mother has a greater right over a child after she is divorced by her husband as the mother is closer to the child and loves it with a greater intensity than anyone else including the father." Maqdisi also says the welfare of the child should be the only criterion in deciding the *hizanat* and anything that harms the child and his/ her religion should not be permitted by law. Imam Shafii (1987) holds a similar view. He says the mother has a greater right over her child and it is the question of the welfare of the child and not merely a parent's right over the child, which should be the deciding factor in the matter of *hizanat*.

All the above opinions of the Prophet (pbuh) and those of the other authorities lead us to the inevitable conclusion that in the matter of *hizanat* the primary consideration under Islamic law is the welfare of the child. Since the mother is more capable of looking after the child she has a greater right over the child. However, each case should be decided on the basis of its own special circumstances and if the father is better suited to look after the child, he should be preferred to the mother. In cases where the mother is disqualified (under the circumstances previously mentioned), custody should be given to the father or in his absence to the relatives of the mother. The primary consideration should always be the welfare of the child. However, on the question of disqualification, the father should be treated in the same way as the mother. If the child can make a choice themselves, he/she should always be given the right to decide. In any case, the welfare of the child being the ultimate criteria, the mother does not automatically lose her right of *hizanat* of her child even when she is disqualified by her marriage to another person.

In view of the above, it can be stated without any fear of contradiction that Islamic law grants women equal if not superior rights when compared with men in the matter of *hizanat* despite the Quran being noncommittal on this subject in favor or against the members of either sex.

On the question of access to children by either parent, both the Quran and the Hadith are silent. Islamic jurists have also not been interested in this subject. Perhaps the silence of the Quran and that of the Hadith on this topic coupled with very limited custody allowed to the mother by the Shariah are behind the disinterest of the jurists. Without guidance from the Shariah on this matter, the courts on the Indian subcontinent (India, Pakistan, and Bangladesh) have followed the precedents of the courts on the question of access to non-Muslim children and applied the same for Muslim children. Dealing briefly with the right of the mother to have access to Muslim children in Pakistan (and Bangladesh) Shawkat Mahmood stated the following: "The Court may direct that the father shall allow the mother to have access to the children and to let them be with her by allowing her either to visit them in the house of the (child's) father or to call them for short periods to herself at any other place within a reasonable distance from the residence of the father and within the jurisdiction of the Court. In the event of the father's failure to comply with these conditions, the mother shall be entitled to seek remedy from the Court." (PLD 1958 Karachi 150)

9

Financial and Economic Provisions for Women in Islamic Law

WOMEN'S RIGHTS OF INHERITANCE

The following are Quranic verses regarding women's rights of inheritance and their rights in the will of a testator from whom they can also inherit:

- "God (thus) directs you as regards your children's (inheritance): to the male, a portion equal to that of two females; if only daughters, two or more, their share is two thirds of the inheritance; if only one, her share is a half. For parents a sixth share of the inheritance to each, if the deceased left children; if no children, and the parents are the (only) heirs, the mother has a third; if the deceased left brothers (or sisters) the mother has a sixth. (The distribution in all cases is) after the payment of legacies and debts. You know not whether your parents or your children are nearest to you in benefit. These are settled portions ordained by God. And God is All-Knowing, All-Wise." (4:11)

- "In what your wives leave, your share is a half, if they leave no child; but if they leave a child, you get a fourth; after payment of legacies and debts. In what you leave, their share is a fourth, if you leave no child; but if you leave a child, they get an eighth; after payment of legacies and debts. If the man or woman whose inheritance is in question, has left neither ascendants or descendants, but has left a brother or a sister, each one of the two gets a sixth;

but if more than two, they share in a third; after payments of legacies and debts; so that no loss is caused (to anyone). Thus it is ordained by God; And God is All-Knowing, Most Forbearing." (4:12)

- "They ask you for a legal decision. Say: God directs (thus) about those who leave no descendants or ascendants as heirs. If it is a man that dies, leaving a sister but no child, she shall have half the inheritance: if (such a deceased was) a woman, who left no child, her brother takes her inheritance: if there are two sisters, they shall have two-thirds of the inheritance (between them): if there are brothers and sisters, (they share), the male having twice the share of the female. Thus does God make clear to you (His law), lest you err. And God has Knowledge of all things." (4:176)

- "From what is left by parents and those nearest related there is a share for men and a share for women, whether the property be small or large—a determinate share.

   But if at the time of division other relatives, or orphans, or poor are present, feed them out of the (property), and speak to them words of kindness and justice." (4:7–8)

- "It is prescribed, when death approaches any of you, if he leave any goods, that he make a bequest to parents and next of kin, according to reasonable usage; this is due from the God fearing." (2:180)

- "If anyone changes the bequest after hearing it, the guilt shall be on those who make the change. For God hears and knows (all things)." (2:181)

- "But if anyone fears partiality or wrong doing on the part of the testator, and makes peace between them (the parties concerned), there is no wrong in him: For God is Oft-forgiving, Most Merciful." (2:182)

- "O you who believe! When death approaches any of you, (take) witnesses among yourselves when making bequests—two just men of your own (brotherhood) or others from outside if you are journeying through the earth, and the chance of death befalls you (thus). If you doubt (their truth), detain them both after prayer, and let them swear by God: We wish not in this for any worldly gain, even though the (beneficiary) be our near relation. We shall hide not the evidence before God: if we do, then behold! The sin be upon us!'" (5:109)

Verses 4:11, 4:12, and 4:176 deal with specific shares of the heirs and 4:7 deals generally with the rights of men and women to the shares in the inheritance. Verse 4:8 asks the Muslims to give special consideration and shares of the inheritance to any relatives, orphans, and needy over and above the specified shares in 4:11, 4:12, and 4:176 at the time of division of the property of the deceased. Verses 2:180, 2:181, 2:182, and 5:109 deal with the rules of bequest in Islam.

With regard to the shares of the female relatives in the inheritance from the deceased, as mentioned in 4:11, 4:12, and 4:176, it is clear they have been allotted a half share of what their male counterparts have been allotted. Thus, a daughter gets half of what a son gets, a brother receives double shares compared to his sister, and the share of the surviving wife is half of what a surviving husband would receive. Islamic jurists have given many explanations and have tried to justify this apparent discrimination between male and female in the sphere of inheritance. We must appreciate that inheritance is very dependent on the social and economic structure of a particular society and therefore we must look at pre-Islamic Arabian rules of inheritance, which although not very clear, were basically dependent on relationship and oath. Keeping aside the rare cases of establishing blood relationship by oath, the criteria of relationship relied on by pre-Islamic Arabs was mainly agnatic relationship ignoring the relationship of the cognates or their successors. Thus, male relatives who took part in battles and captured loot were generally entitled to inherit property, while female relatives were excluded. Verses 4:11, 4:12, and 4:176 gave specific shares in inheritance to women for the first time. Razi (n.d.) informs us about the context of the revelation of 4:11 of the Quran. According to him the issue of women's right of inheritance came to the forefront when the brother of S'ad bin Rabi took away the entire property of the martyred S'ad depriving the wife and daughter of S'ad. When S'ad's wife complained about this to the Prophet (pbuh) he simply said that God would decide in this matter. Soon after, 4:11 was revealed and the Prophet (pbuh) ordered S'ad's brother to pay two-thirds of the property to two daughters of S'ad, one-eighth of the property to S'ad's widow, and keep the remainder himself (the brother).

Apart from the sociological and economic context of the half shares for women in inheritance, two other arguments are advanced justifying this discrimination against women relatives. First, the wife is to be looked after by her husband even if she is wealthy enough to look after herself. This principle is derived from verse 65:6–7 of the Quran. The second justification for a woman's half share was advanced by the tenth and eleventh century intellectuals of *Ikhwanus Safa*. They argued that the half share received by women from their inheritance along with their right of *mahr* (dower) from their husbands sanctioned by 4:4 of the Quran would place them on an equal footing with their male counterparts so far as the acquisition of wealth is concerned. (Engineer 1992) However, the ideal situation pictured or visualized by the authors of *Ikhwanus Safa* and their supporters may not be the same in reality. In many cases, the wife's right of *mahr* is not enough compensation for her receiving only a half share of the inheritance compared with her male counterpart. The obvious question which comes to mind is what happens if the daughter cannot marry for some reason and even if she is married she is not well provided for through her own means or through her husband's wealth. In such special cases near relatives can make a notional or constructive bequest in her favor as prescribed by verse 4:8 as if the testator himself made the said bequest before his/her death. The Zahiri jurist, Ibne Hazm, considered it was positively obligatory on the part of the deceased to make bequests in favor of near relatives in need. Hazm further held that such provisions could be enforced by the court if the deceased had failed to perform his duty (Anderson & Coulson n.d.). It is therefore necessary to examine more thoroughly the provisions of 2:180, 2:181, 2:182, and 5:109 that deal with bequests by the testator giving additional rights to the property of the deceased, apart from the Quranic shares. First, it is clear from the wording of both 2:180 and 2:181 that the Quran gives the testator an unfettered right to dispose of his/her property by bequest or will to anyone he/she chooses. Second, 4:8 specifically asks Muslims to make a constructive bequest to relatives, orphans, and the needy if the deceased had failed to make provisions for these classes of people before his/her death. Third, 2:181 of the Quran prohibits anyone who knows about the will from changing its provisions and if one does so (change the will) after knowing about it he/she will be guilty. Fourth, both 4:11 and 4:12 make provisions for the Quranic sharers from the residue of the estate after the payment of bequests and debt. *Mahr* of the wife is a debt having priority over any debt or liabilities incurred after the date of marriage.

Despite the clear wording of 4:8, 2:180, and 2:181, Islamic jurists invented a rule denying anybody the right to receive more than one-third of the residue of a deceased Muslim's estate through bequest, and any bequest or will giving anybody a share of the deceased's testator's estate exceeding one-third could be effected only with the consent of the testator's Quranic heirs. (Fyzee 1964) An additional restriction on legacy or bequest by all four Sunni schools of law and by the Fatimi school is the maxim, "No bequest to an heir." These two rules are strictly followed in India, Pakistan, and Bangladesh. With regard to the second restriction, it is quite clear the Sunnis and the Fatimids are acting in opposition to 2:180 of the Quran. The Sunnis made the second rule on the basis of an alleged sentence in the Prophet's (pbuh) Farewell Pilgrimage address to the effect that "God had given to everyone his due, therefore there shall be no bequest to one who is entitled to inherit" (Ali n.d.). Bukhari quoutes another Hadith which limits bequests to one-third of the estate (B 23:36). However, as it has been emphasized repeatedly that no Hadith can cancel any Quranic verse, Sunni jurists are wrong when they restrict Muslims from bequeathing more than one-third of their estate, despite the prohibitive rule of this alleged Hadith. We have seen that 2:180 and 2:181 put no restrictions in bequeathing the whole or more than one third of the estate. Without any support either from the Quran, the Hadith, or from the history of Islam, some jurists of Islam argue 2:180 was abrogated. Citing several Hadiths and historical incidents, Muhammad Ali (1950) establishes that neither the Prophet (pbuh) nor his disciples (including Hazrat Ayesha and Caliph Ali) considered that verse 2:180 was abrogated. According to Muhammed Ali (1951) the precondition of making a bequest was abundant wealth (*taraka khaira*). Ali also states that 2:180 sanctions bequests only for charitable purpose or for relatives who could not inherit under 4:11 of the Quran. While Muhammad Ali is correct about 2:180 not being abrogated, he is wrong in holding that the bequest must have the two preconditions as stated by him. First, 2:180 does not forbid a bequest to near relatives or next of kin and second, *taraka khaira* does not necessarily mean 'leaving a large property' but means 'leaving of property or good things. Parvez (1979) points out it is wrong to think a person cannot make a will reducing the shares of the Quranic sharers of his property. Parvez opines that it is definitely wrong for Islamic jurists to maintain a person cannot make a will as this is in opposition to the definite view of the Quran. Besides, the expression '*min badi wasiyyatin yusi biha*' (after the payment of legacies) in both 4:11 and 4:12 clearly indicate the inheritor will get what is left after payment of the legacies. With regard to the alleged abrogation of 2:180–182, Abu Bakr Jassas (1347 AH) informs us that along with 18 obligations in the 5th Sura (al-Maida), the verses on bequests (5:106–108) have not been abrogated and therefore, by inference, 2:180–182 are also not abrogated. Imam Hasan Basri supports this view. Moulana Usmani (1980) is also of the opinion that 2:180 was not abrogated.

Verse 2:182 deals with the partiality or wrongdoing on the part of a testator. Abdullah Yusuf Ali (1946) suggests that if a testator is partial to one heir at the expense of another, or does anything wrongful (including depriving a lawful creditor) those who are witnesses to his oral disposition may change it in two ways. First, the witness can persuade the testator to change his bequest and if that fails, he can consult with the interested parties and ask them to agree to an equitable arrangement as suggested by 2:182. However, one must be aware that if the parties concerned cannot come to an arrangement regarding the will, that is the end of the matter and the provisions of the will take effect. Further, if the parties are not acting in good faith, changing of the provisions of a will is a crime, as it is under all law.

MAINTENANCE OF THE WIFE BY THE HUSBAND AND HIS ESTATE

Maintenance of the Wife by the Husband during Marriage

In Islamic terminology, the equivalent expression for maintenance is '*nafaqa*' and includes food, clothing, and lodging. The responsibilities for the maintenance of dependents are held through marriage and relationship. At present, we are concerned about the relationships through marriage. The maintenance of wife and children is the primary obligation of the husband and of the father, respectively. According to Tyabji (1940), in the list of recipients of maintenance from her husband the wife comes first, although she may have the means to maintain herself, and although her husband may be without means. A husband's duty to maintain his wife arises from 4:34 that says, "Men are the protectors and maintainers of women, because God has given the one more (strength) than the other, and because they support them from their means" (4:34). The husband's duty of maintenance starts with his wife's puberty and according to Islamic jurists, continues provided she is obedient and allows him full access at all lawful times. Apart from this legal (Islamic) obligation to maintain his wife, a husband may have an additional obligation to give special allowance (*kharch-i-pandan*), to the wife as part of a stipulation in the marriage contract. Two other verses of the Quran (65:6 and 65:7) also emphasize the husband's duty to maintain the wife. These are as follows:

- "Let the women live (in iddat) in the same style as you live according to your means..." (65:6)

- "Let the man of means spend according to his means: and then man whose resources are restricted, let him spend according to what God has given him . . . " (65:7)

Muhammad Ali (1950) is of the opinion that these two verses apply to the maintenance of the wife by the husband in all circumstances, whereas Abdullah Yusuf Ali translates 65:6 by including in parenthesis the words "in Iddat" after the expression "let the woman live" thereby suggesting 65:6 is confined to the cases of divorced women in course of her *iddat* period. There is no doubt Yusuf Ali was wrong in limiting the maintenance of the wife to the *iddat* period, as his inclusion of the expression in *iddat* in 65:6 in parenthesis is definitely not mentioned in the original words of the Quran in 65:6. The Quran always urges the husband to treat his wife kindly (2:229) and not treat her harshly (4:14). The Prophet (pbuh) laid emphasis on the good treatment towards wives when he said, "The most excellent of you is he who is best in his treatment of his wife" (M 13:11). Muhammad Ali (1950) says, "The wife must help the husband even in the field of labour if she can do it, and the husband must help the wife in household duties. The wife is not bound to give personal service including cooking."

The right of the maintenance of the wife continues during the marriage and even after divorce but during the *iddat* period. However, this right of maintenance ceases on the death of her husband. Imam Malik (1981) and Imam Shafii (1987) both opine that the husband's inability, refusal, or neglect to maintain his wife is proper grounds for the dissolution of the marriage. But Hanafi law does not give any right of the dissolution of the marriage on either of these grounds.

Maintenance of a Divorced Woman During and After the *Iddat* Period

The Quran has laid down the principle of the maintenance of the divorced women in 2:241 and the details of such maintenance are given in 65:6 and 65:7. Thus, the Quran says:

- "For divorced women maintenance (should be provided) on a reasonable (scale). This is a duty on the righteous."(2:241)

- "Let the women live (in *iddat*) in the same style as you live, according to your means: annoy them not, so as to restrict them. And if they carry (life in their wombs), then spend (your substance) on them until they deliver their burden: and if they suckle your (off-spring), give them their recompense: and take mutual counsel together, according to what is just and reasonable. And if you find yourselves in difficulties, let another woman suckle (the child) on the (father's) behalf." (65:6)

- "Let the man of means spend according to his means: and the man whose resources are restricted, let him spend according to what god has given him. God puts no burden on any person beyond what he has given him. After a difficulty God will soon grant relief." (65:7)

While asking husbands to pay maintenance to their divorced wives according to their own standards of life, the Quran does not fix any time limit for maintenance, does not mention the amount of maintenance or the period of maintenance. The majority of classical jurists of Islamic law interpreted 2:241 to mean that maintenance is limited to the period of *iddat* and is the Islamic law for the maintenance of divorced women in the Indian subcontinent. However, in the leading case of Shah Bano, the Supreme Court of India awarded maintenance to Shah Bano beyond the period of *iddat*. The court relied on the translation of 2:241 by Yusuf Ali. This decision has been criticized by conservative Muslim leaders of India as against the law of God as given in the Quran. However, verse 2:241 neither mentions any time limit nor any specific amount for the maintenance of the divorced woman. '*Mataa*' and '*bil maruf*' are the two key expressions in 2:241. These expressions have been translated and interpreted by various authors in different ways. According to Abdullah Yusuf Ali (1946), *mataa* means 'maintenance' and *maruf* means 'reasonable scale'. Muhammad Ali (1951) translates them as 'provisions made in kindness.' Muhammad Asad (1984) translates *mataa* as 'maintenance' and *maruf* as 'goodly manner'. Imam Hasan Basri opines that there is no time limit regarding payment of maintenance and that it should be paid according to one's capacity (Ahmed n.d.). According to a classical Arabic lexicon, *Lisan al-Arabi*, *mataa* has no time limit as Allah has not fixed any time limit for it and has only enjoined the payment of maintenance (Ahmed n.d.). Imam Raghib (1485) defines *mataa* (in 2:241) as something given for the period of *iddat*.

Allama Nujaym (n.d.), a Hanafi jurist, discusses the conflicting views of Hanafi jurists. He tells us that according to Imam Muhammad a husband is not required to pay maintenance to his divorced wife. But Imam Abu Yusuf opines that a husband would have to pay maintenance even after divorcing her. Nujaym agrees with the consensus of the jurists; a woman not properly maintained by her husband can knock at the door of the court and have her maintenance allowance fixed. The husband would be bound to pay the fixed amount to his wife regularly. Discussing the Shah Bano case, Professor Rafiullah Shihab (1986) opined that if a wife is not properly maintained by her husband, she can have her maintenance allowance granted through the court. This allowance would be awarded to her not only during her married life but also after divorce.

Maintenance of Widows from a Husband's Estate or Will

The Quran does not mention a widow's right of maintenance and as the right of inheritance is activated immediately on the husband's death, a widow is not entitled to the maintenance during the *iddat* period after the husband's death. However, the Quran has provided a special right for the widow by asking the husband to leave a will in favor of his surviving wife. Thus the Quran says, "Those of you who die and leave widows should bequeath for their widows a year's maintenance and residence; but if they leave (the residence), there is no blame on you for what they do with themselves, provided it is reasonable. And God is Exalted in Power, Wise" (2:240).

However, the problem arises when the deceased husband fails to provide maintenance to his wife by a will. In such cases focus should be placed on the intent and purpose of 2:240 of the Quran, which encourages a provision of maintenance for the widow through the will of the deceased husband. By the method of *ijtihad*, a will could be presumed to be made and in the absence of a real will a 'constructive will' should be included as a testamentary provision by the deceased husband and the said 'constructive will' should give maintenance to the wife on the same basis as maintenance given to a divorced woman. If she happens to carry the child of the deceased husband or suckle the child of the deceased, she should receive the same benefit as received by a divorced women under 65:6 of the Quran.

A WOMAN'S RIGHT OF DOWER *(MAHR)*

Apart from the right of inheritance, the right of being a beneficiary in a will, and the right of maintenance from their husbands, married Muslim women have a special right of dower (*mahr*) from their husbands. While defining dower in Abdul Kadir versus Salima (AIR 1886–8 Allahabad 149, 157), Mr. Justice Mahmood states, "Dower, under the Muhammadan Law, is a sum of money or other property promised by the husband to be paid or delivered to the wife in consideration of the marriage, and even where no dower is fixed or mentioned at the marriage ceremony, the law confers the right of dower upon the wife." According to Lord Parker, "The dower ranks as a debt, and the wife is entitled along with the other creditors to have it satisfied on the death of the husband out of his estate" (Hamira Bibi versus Zubaida Bibi referred to by Justice Khaliluzzaman, in Kaporechand versus Kadar Unnissa SCR 1950 747, 751).

The following verses of the Quran refer to dower (*mahr*):

- "And give the women (on marriage) their dower as a free gift; but if they, of their own good pleasure, remit any part of it to you, take it and enjoy it with right good cheer." (4:4)

- "But if you decide to take one wife in place of another, even if you had given the latter a whole treasure for dower, take not the least bit of it back; would you take it by slander and a manifest wrong?
  And how could you take it when you have gone in unto each other, and they have taken from you a solemn covenant?" (4:20–21)

- " . . . seeing that you derive benefit from them (the wives) give them their dowers as prescribed . . . " (4:24)

- "There is no blame on you if you divorce women before consummation or the fixation of their dower; but bestow on them (a suitable gift), the wealthy according to his means, and the poor according to his means—a gift of reasonable amount is due from those who wish to do the right thing.
  And if you divorce them before consummation, but after the fixation of a dower for them, then the half of the dower (is due to them), unless they remit it or (the man's half) is remitted by him in whose hands is the marriage tie; and the remission (of the man's half) is the nearest to righteousness. And do not forget liberality between yourselves. For God sees well all that you do." (2:236–237)

- "O you who believe! When you marry believing women, and then divorce them before you have touched them, no period of iddat have you to count in respect of them: so give them a present, and set them free in a handsome manner." (33:49)

Let us look at some comments made by commentators on these verses. Various interpretations of various expressions in the above Quranic verses are worth mentioning here. The expression '*saduqut*' (plural of *saduqah* from *sidq* meaning truth) is used for dower in 4:4. According to Muhammad Ali (1951), *saduqat* is different from the expression *sadaqah* (meaning charity) which also comes from the same root. Other words used for dower are *mahr*, *suduq*, and *nahlah* (derived from *nahl* or honey). In verse 2:237, reference is made to "him in whose hands is the marriage tie." Abdullah Yusuf Ali (1946) informs us that the Hanafis consider this expression refers to the husband, as it is the husband who can dissolve the marriage by *talaq*. Abdullah Yusuf Ali (1946), agreeing with some other commentators of the Quran thinks that the expression, "So give them a present" in 33:49 refers to a gift or present in addition to the half dower mentioned in 2:237. He also states that if the dower had not been fixed, this present would be larger absorbing the gift mentioned in 2:236.

The Quran does not specify any amount of *mahr*. It is the bride's right to demand as much *mahr* as she desires at the time of marriage. It could be minimal or it could be a great amount. A Hadith of the Prophet (pbuh) tells us that when the husband has no capacity to pay, it could be nominal (e.g. an iron ring or teaching of lessons) (Bukhari 1973). On the other hand, *mahr* could be a substantial amount, even a whole treasure as mentioned in verse 4:20 of the Quran. Although Hanafi jurists have decided the minimum dower should be ten dirhams and the Maliki jurists opined the minimum dower should be three dirhams, the Prophet's (pbuh) Hadith quoted above contradicts these opinions. On the other hand, fixing the maximum limit of dower recommended by some jurists cannot be supported as rational. Fyzee (1964) states that a proper dower should be fixed on the basis of the social position of her father's family, as well as her own social position without any account being taken of the husband's social position and means. *The Hedaya* lays down the rule that her "age, beauty, fortune, understanding and virtue must be taken into consideration." However, as mentioned, a husband without any capacity to pay a proper dower should pay only a nominal amount. The author of *The Hedaya* considers that marriage without the mention of dower, or with a condition there should be no dower, is also valid (al-Marghinani 1982). This opinion of *The Hedaya* is contrary to the Quran as the Quran is very specific about the *mahr* being an integral part of the marriage. In fact, if no *mahr* has been fixed or mentioned at the time of marriage, *mahr-i-mithl* (dower of the like or proposed dower) is to be paid by the husband. If the *mahr* is fixed at the time of marriage it is called *al-mahr ul musamma* or *al-mahr ul aqd*. As opposed to al-Marghinani, Maudoodi (1987) holds the opinion every Muslim must clear his dower debt and if a husband dies without paying his wife's dower, it becomes a debt of the deceased's estate. Maudoodi went on to comment that the Prophet (pbuh) refused to offer funeral prayers for a Muslim who had not paid a dower to his widow. The dower is confirmed by (a) consummation of the marriage, (b) *khilwat-e-sahiha* (valid retirement), or (c) the death of either the husband or the wife. Imam Abu Hanifa says that even a moment spent together would result in the full payment of the dower (Usmani 1980). The part of the *mahr*, which is paid at the time of the marriage, is called *mahr-i-muajjal* (immediately paid portion of *mahr*) and the part of *mahr*, which is to be paid at a later date or at the time of divorce or death of either spouse is called *mahr-i-muwajjal* (deferred portion of the dower).

Finally, the Quran commands that women should not be forced to return the part of dower given to them as the Quran says, ". . . Nor you (believers) should treat them (wives) with harshness, that you may take away part of the dower you have given them—except where they have been guilty of open lewdness; on the contrary live with them on a footing of kindness and equity. . ." (4:19). Apart from giving financial and economic benefit to Muslim women, the Quran ensures a woman's earnings on an equal footing with men. As the Quran says, ". . . to men is allotted what they earn, and to women what they earn . . ." (4:32).

10

Rules Regarding Women as
Witnesses in Islamic Law

Despite being fair to women witnesses, Islamic law is unjustly criticized
by Western scholars for alleged discrimination of women as witnesses and
they criticize Islamic law for giving less value to a woman's evidence.
Unfortunately, conservative Muslim jurists help critics of Islamic law by
asserting that indeed it demands two women witnesses in lieu of one male
witness. A thorough and critical analysis of the Quranic provisions will
clearly show this is not the case. The following are Quranic verses regarding evidence and witnesses relevant to this topic:

- "O you who believe! When you deal with each other, in transactions involving future obligations in a fixed period of time, reduce
  them to writing. Let a scribe write down faithfully as between the
  parties; let not the scribe refuse to write: as God has taught him,
  so let him write. Let him who incurs the liability dictate, but let
  him fear his Lord God, and not diminish aught of what he owes.
  If the party liable is mentally deficient, or weak, or unable himself
  to dictate, let his guardian dictate faithfully. And get two witnesses, out of your own men, and if there are not two men, then
  a man and two women, such as you choose, for witnesses, so that
  if one of them errs, the other can remind her. The witnesses should
  not refuse when they are called on (for evidence). Disdain not to
  reduce to writing (your contract) for a future period, whether it be
  small or big: it is juster in the sight of God, more suitable as

evidence, and more convenient to prevent doubts among your-selves. But if it be a transaction which you carry out on the spot among yourselves there is no blame on you if you reduce it not to writing. But take witnesses whenever you make a commercial con-tract; and let neither scribe nor witness suffer harm. If you do (such harm), it would be wickedness in you. So fear God; for it is God that teaches you. and God is well acquainted with all things.

If you are on a journey, and cannot find a scribe, a pledge with possession (may serve the purpose). And if one of you deposits a thing on trust with another, let the trustee (faithfully) discharge his trust, and let him fear his Lord. Conceal not evidence; for whoever conceals it—his heart is tainted with sin. And God knows all that you do." (2:282–283)

- "O you who believe! When death approaches any of you, (take) witnesses among yourselves when making bequests—*two just men of your own (brotherhood)*—or others from outside if you are jour-neying through the earth, and the chance of death befalls you (thus). If you doubt (their truth), detain them both after prayer, and let them both swear by God: 'We wish not in this for any worldly gain, even though the (beneficiary) be our near relation: we shall hide not the evidence before God: if we do, then behold! The sin be upon us!'" (5:109—Yusuf Ali's translation)

  "O you who believe, call to witness between you, when death draws nigh to one of you, at the time of making the will, *two just persons from among you,* or two others from among others than you, if you are traveling in the land and the calamity of death befalls you. You should detain them after prayer. Then if you doubt (them), they shall both swear by Allah (saying): we will not take for it a price, though there be a relative nor will we hide the testimony of Allah, for then certainly we shall be sinners." (5:106—Muhammad Ali's translation)

- "But if it gets known that these two were guilty of the sin (of perjury), let two others stand forth in their places – nearest in kin from among those who claim a lawful right. Let them swear by God: 'We affirm that our witness is truer than that of those two, and that we have not trespassed (beyond the truth): if we did, behold, the wrong be upon us!

  That is most suitable: that they may give the evidence in its true nature and shape, or else they would fear that other oaths would be taken after their oaths. But fear God, and listen (to his counsel); for God guides not a rebellious people." (5:110–111)

• "If any of your women are guilty of lewdness, take the evidence of four (reliable) witnesses from amongst you against them; and if they testify, confine them to houses until death do claim them, or God ordain for them some (other) way." (4:15)

• "And those who launch a charge against chaste women, and produce not four witnesses (to support their allegations)—flog them with eighty stripes; and reject their evidence ever after: for such men are wicked transgressors." (24:4)

• "And for those who launch a charge against their spouses, and have (in support) no evidence but their own—their solitary evidence (can be received) if they bear witness four times (with an oath) by God that they are solemnly telling the truth.

And the fifth (oath) should be that they solemnly invoke the curse of God on themselves if they tell a lie.

But it would avert the punishment from the wife, if she bears witness four times (with an oath) by God, that (her husband) is telling a lie.

And the fifth (oath) should be that she solemnly invokes the wrath of God on herself if (her accuser) is telling the truth." (24:6–9)

• "Why did not the believers—men and women—when they heard of the affair—put the best construction on it in their own minds and say, 'This (charge) is an obvious lie?'

Why did they not bring four witnesses to prove it? When they have not brought the witnesses, such men in the sight of God (stand forth) themselves as liars."(24:12–13)

• "Thus when they fulfil their term appointed, either take them back on equitable terms or part with them on equitable terms; and take for witnesses two persons from among you, endued with justice, and establish the evidence (as) before God. Such is the admonition given to him who believes in God and the Last Day. And for those who fear God, He (ever) prepares a way out." (65:2)

Let us look at these verses in detail. Verse 2:282 of the Quran relates to transactions or contracts for future obligations and only this verse refers to two women witnesses being necessary, if instead of two male witnesses only one male is available for being witness. Verse 2:283 refers to transactions on a journey when no scribe is available to write it down and ask witnesses not to conceal evidence. Verse 5:109 (5:106 in Muhammad Ali's translation) relates to witnesses for making bequests. A particular section of this verse (italicized in the text of the verse above) needs a careful analysis as it has been translated in different ways. Abdullah Yusuf Ali (1946) wrongly translates the expression *asnanayzawadlay* as 'two just men' although *asnanay* means 'two persons.' Muhammad Ali (1951) correctly translates the expression as 'two just persons.' The expression *minkum* does not mean 'of your own (brotherhood)' as Yusuf Ali translates. In fact, by putting the word brotherhood in parenthesis, Yusuf Ali indirectly admits the Quran does not mention brotherhood in this verse. Muhammad Ali correctly translates *minkum* as 'from among you.' Therefore, in reality, there is no mention about the sex of the witness in this verse. Verses 5:110 and 5:111 relate to witnesses for a bequest in cases where the two original witnesses are known to be guilty of the sin of perjury. The verse recommends the acceptance of two other witnesses in their place and no mention is made here about the sex of the witnesses. Verse 4:15 relates to witnesses against women charged of lewdness and asks for taking the evidence of four reliable witnesses 'from among you.' The sex of the witnesses is not mentioned here. Verse 24:4 relates to punishment of the accusers of chaste women who fail to produce four witnesses (to support their allegations). Again no sex of witnesses is mentioned. Verses 24:6–9 deal with allegations against a wife by her husband unsupported by any witnesses except the husband. The husband is asked in such cases to state four times on oath to God he is telling the truth invoking the curse of God if he is not telling the truth. Similarly, a wife can avert punishment for the alleged sin if she states four times on oath to God she is telling the truth invoking the curse of God if her husband is telling the truth. Verses 24:12–13 ask believers to consider the charge as a lie and the accusing husband as a liar in the sight of God if he fails to bring four independent witnesses. Again, the sex of the witnesses is not mentioned. Verse 65:2 relates to the necessity of two witnesses at the time of the husband taking back his wife or parting with her at the end of the *iddat* period. Again, the sex of the two witnesses is not mentioned.

It appears the only verse that supports the allegation of the inferior status of women as witnesses is 2:282. But closer scrutiny of 2:282 will clarify its real position. First, the application of 2:282 is confined only to financial contracts as there is no mention of any other kind of contract in 2:282. Second, the reason for substituting two women for one male witness was necessary because women were less familiar with financial matters at the time of the revelation of 2:282 in seventh century A.D. Arabia. On the question of women's inferior status as witnesses mentioned in 2:282, various commentators of 2:282 attempt to explain the disparity of treatment by the Quran giving an inferior position to women witnesses in financial contracts. Muhammad Asad (1980) justifies this disparity by commenting that, according to him, women witnesses are less familiar with business procedures than men and therefore are more liable to make mistakes in these matters. Muhammad Abduh states a similar view. With respect, I submit this justification of the disparity in 2:282 is hardly tenable in modern times. Fazlur Rahman (1980) gives a less objectionable justification of this disparity in 2:282. According to Rahman, the inferior position of women witnesses is because women had weaker powers of memory than men in financial matters. Rahman further states that when women become conversant in financial matters their evidence can equal that of men. It appears that if Fazlur Rahman's recommendation for more conversant women is accepted the disparity of 2:282 vanishes in modern society. However, the most acceptable explanation of the disparity against women is forwarded by Asghar Ali Engineer (1992) who believes the provision of 2:282 is only recommendary and not obligatory. Quoting another section of 2:282, which says, "Let a scribe record it in writing between you in equity." Engineer justifies the recommendation of the Quran by commenting that to be fair to both creditors and the debtors, the Quran recommends the contract be written properly and supported only by qualified witnesses. While discussing fairness (or otherwise) to women in the recommendation of 2:282, one must remember that only one woman witness among the two women is required to give evidence although two women witnesses substitute for one male witness. The provision of 2:282 is "if one of them errs, the other can remind her."

Regarding the evidence of women witnesses generally, a disciple of Ibn Taymiyah, Ibn Qayyim (n.d.) observes neither the Quran nor the Hadith made this rule. Qayyim also states that this provision does not mean that if there are less than two female witnesses, no judgment can be based on the evidence of one women witness. In a case of *hadd* (punishment prescribed by the Quran), Bukhari (1973) states the Prophet (pbuh) passed sentence on the basis of a woman's evidence. Similarly, on the question of *qisas* most of the companions of the Prophet (pbuh) demanded *qisas* on the murderers of Caliph Usman on the solitary evidence of Naila, Usman's wife. Jassas (1347 AH) mentions Imam Zahri's opinion that a woman's evidence is acceptable in all matters where there is no other evidence. Imam Taymiyyah agrees with the view of Imam

Zahri and reasons that if an offence is committed in a bathing place where only women are present, and this offence is punishable by *hadd*, then the case will be decided on the woman's evidence alone (Engineer 1992). This is also the opinion of Imam Ahmad Ibn Hanbal. Imam Shafii (n.d.) goes to another extreme and states that in matters connected with woman (e.g. childbirth), only women's evidence is acceptable and no man is required to give evidence with them. Imam Zahri agrees with this view.

In recent times, the courts on the Indian subcontinent have strengthened the position of women witnesses. In the case of Fida Hussain versus Naseem Akhtar in the Lahore High Court in Pakistan, Justice Aftab Hussain had to deal with the question of the competence of a woman witness without a male witness. Justice Hussain held that Islam does not fix any particular number of witnesses to prove a case as the Prophet (pbuh) had decided on the evidence of either of the following categories of witnesses:

1. (on) the evidence of a woman plaintiff

2. (on) the evidence of a female witness

3. (on) the evidence produced by both parties

4. (on) the evidence of witness and oath (Yamin) of the plaintiff

5. (on) the oath of the defendant and the evidence of two or more witnesses

With his authority as a former chief justice of the Federal Shariat Court of Pakistan, Justice Aftab Hussain (1987) concluded the admissibility and competence of a woman witness (for or against her) has never been debarred by the Quran and the Hadith.

In view of the above discussion, it is my considered opinion, female witnesses are in no way inferior to male witnesses according to Islamic law. Even in matters of financial contracts, in the changed circumstances of the modern world, female witnesses should be treated on an equal footing with male witnesses as the recommendations made in 2:282 on financial contracts is no longer obligatory on Muslims.

11

Rules Regarding the Seclusion
of Women (Purdah)

One of the most controversial and difficult topics a Muslim confronts in his social life is the subject of purdah in Islam. On the one hand we have the present system of purdah as practiced by Muslims in the present time, particularly by the Muslims coming from the Indian subcontinent. On the other hand, we have various Quranic and Hadith regulations and injunctions which provide the rules and methods Muslims are obliged to follow with regard to their dress, privacy, and manners while coming across the members of the opposite sex. A careful consideration of the duties and obligations which Muslims are asked to follow by the Quran and authentic Hadiths of the Prophet Muhammad (pbuh) show the so-called system of purdah, as we know it today, has very little to do with Islam. The study of Islamic history from the time of the Prophet (pbuh) until today reveals the shocking truth that the present purdah system owes its origin to reactionary Muslim rulers in various countries and by the regulators of Muslim society who were undoubtedly influenced by the societies and cultures with whom they came into contact after the conquest of Iran, parts of the Byzantine empire, and India. It is therefore appropriate to discuss first these historical factors that introduced the purdah system in Muslim society, as we know today.

The Arab conquest of Persia (present day Iran) brought Muslims into close contact with Iranian civilization, its culture, and its practices that obviously had a profound influence on Arab Muslims. Even after their conversion to Islam, most Iranians retained traditional dress, such as *shalwar* and *sherwani*, and continued their old system of purdah or seclusion. Similar to Iranian women, Roman and Greek women of the Byzantian territories occupied by the Muslims, covered their face, hands, and in fact, their whole body when coming out of their homes. Contact with Greeks, Romans, and other subjects of the erstwhile Byzantine Empire had a deep influence on Arab Muslim society. This influence became stronger when many of these people, particularly slaves and artists, came to the capitals and cities of the Arab empire. Syed Ameer Ali (n.d.), writes in *The Short History of the Saracens*, "Large influx into the capital of slave classes in pursuit of their vocations of dancing and singing gradually led to the segregation of the respectable section of the female community among the Muslim Arabs."

The martyrdom of Hazrat Ali, the fourth Caliph, is a landmark in the history of Islam. With his death, the *khulafae-rashidin* (the Caliphate of the pure Caliphs) came to an end and then began the Umayyad Caliphate with all its undemocratic attitudes, corruption, and deviations from the path of Islam. However, despite these profound changes in Muslim society there was no system of harem among Arab Muslims until the reign of Umayyad Caliph Walid the Second (al-Ispahani 1963). Syed Ameer Ali (n.d.) writes in *The Short History of the Saracens*, "His (Walid the Second's) utter disregard for social conventionalities and the daring and coolness with which he entered into the privacy of the families, compelled the adoption of the safeguards against outside intrusions which once introduced became sanctified into custom. To the uncultured mind, wall and warden appear to afford more effective protection than nobility of sentiment and purity of heart." However, although the seclusion of women and the *harem* were introduced during the time of Walid the Second, the universal acceptance of these customs among Arab Muslims took a considerable amount of time. By the time of the Abbaside Caliph, Mutawakkil (847 A.D.), the system and the custom of the harem and the purdah system (by which the Muslim women were kept in seclusion in a separate part of the household) had a firm grip on Muslim society under Abbaside rule. By then, Muslim women had many restrictions in their movements outside their homes. The Mongol conquest of Baghdad by Hulagu Khan in 1258 A.D. is another turning point in the history of Muslims. The Mongol conquest compelled Muslims to keep their women in seclusion to protect them from the ruthless and lecherous Mongol hordes of Hulagu Khan.

When Muslims conquered India from the Hindus, they found the Hindu custom of the seclusion of women even worse than the Iranians and Byzantians. In India, Hindu women prided themselves in not ever coming into contact with sun rays, as they called themselves '*ashurjampashsha*' (untouched by the sun). It was the influence of Indian Hindus that made the purdah system of Indian Muslims the worst and most restricted form of seclusion of women in the whole of the Muslim world. It was thus that the purdah system gradually crept into Muslim society. Sir Muhammad Sulaiman (1935), the former chief justice of the Allahabad High Court and a great authority on Islamic law and Muslim society, summarized the system of purdah among Indian Muslims with the following words:

"No doubt the extreme Indian form owes its origin to the peculiar circumstances in which a small minority of Muslim invaders in the medieval ages found themselves in the midst of an alien majority. Protection of life and property was not more urgent than the protection of their women. As men had to lead an active outdoor life and could not always remain by the side of their women folk, the only possible course open in that age of battle and brigandage was the shutting up of women in 'zenanas,' thus giving them natural and safe protection. The continued warfare and bloodshed of those times made the purdah system stricter and stricter, until it assumed the form in which we find it today. It was the unfortunate and peculiar condition of the country that made it difficult for Muslim women to go out of their houses, even veiled, and this deprived them of the liberty of movement that their sisters in Arabia, Turkey, Egypt, Persia and Afghanistan and those in North Africa enjoyed. No one can assert that shutting up of women within closed walls is sanctioned by any text or tradition."

On *burkha*, Sir Sulaiman (1935) says, "Its use is only traditional as copied from other nations, and which Muslims gradually exaggerated, giving to it a religious significance. It is therefore clear that Islam cannot be blamed for the attending evils and the social causes of the purdah system observed all over the Indian sub-continent and that the *burkha*, the portable black hole carried by the Muslim women of the Indian sub-continent, has no religious basis whatsoever."

This brief summary of the gradual introduction of purdah among Muslims leads us to the more relevant area of our study. These are the sanctions of the Quran and the Hadith regarding the social position of

Muslim women, her dress, her manners and her behavior, and above all, her mixing or coming into contact with members of the opposite sex. The following are the Quranic verses on purdah, privacy, the way the male and female should conduct their lives in society, and related subjects.

- "Say to the believing men that they should lower their gaze and guard their modesty: that will make for greater purity for them: and God is well acquainted with all that they do." (24:30)

- "And say to the believing women that they should lower their gaze and guard their modesty; that they should not display their beauty and ornaments (*zeenatahunna*) except what (must ordinarily) appear thereof; that they should draw their veils over their bosoms and not display their beauty (*zeenatahunna*) except to their husbands, their fathers, their husbands' fathers, their sons, their husbands' sons, their brothers or their brothers' sons, or their sisters' sons, or their women, or the slaves whom their right hands possess, or male servants free of physical needs, or small children who have no sense of the shame of sex; and that they should not strike their feet in order to draw attention to their hidden ornaments (*zeenatahunna*) and O you believers! You all turn together towards God, that you may attain Bliss." (24:31)

  (In view of the abolition of slavery, the rules regarding seclusion from slaves are obsolete.)

- "O you children of Adam! We have bestowed raiments upon you to cover your shame, as well as to be an adornment to you. But the raiments of righteousness (*taqwa*)—that is the best. Such are among the Signs of God, that they may receive admonition!" (7:26)

- "Say: The things that my Lord has indeed forbidden are shameful deeds whether open or secret; sins and trespasses against truth or reason, assigning of partners to God for which He has given no authority; and saying things about God of which you have no knowledge." (7:33)

- "Say: Come, I will rehearse what God has (really) prohibited you from: not join anything as equal with Him; be good to your parents; kill not your children on a plea of want;—We provide sustenance for you and for them;—come not near to shameful deeds, whether open or secret; take not life which God has made sacred except by way of justice and law: thus He commands you, that you may learn wisdom." (6:151)

- "O consorts of the Prophet! You are not like any of the (other) women: If you do fear God, be not too complacent of speech, lest one in whose heart is a disease should be moved with desire: but you speak a speech (that is) just.

  And stay quietly in your houses, and make not a dazzling display like that of the former Times of Ignorance; and establish Regular prayer and give Regular charity; and obey God and His Apostle. And God only wishes to remove all abomination from you, you members of the Family (*ahl-al-bait*), and to make you pure and spotless." (33:32–33)

From the expression "*ahl-al-bait*" in 33:33, it is clear it refers to the Prophet's (pbuh) wives and the female members of the Prophet's (pbuh) family. The expression *ahl-al-bait* is also used in 11:73 (referring to Abraham's wife) and in 28:12 (referring to the mother of Moses).

- " . . . And when you (believing men) ask (the Prohet's wives) for anything you want, ask them from before a screen: that makes for greater purity for your hearts and for theirs. Nor is it right for you that you should annoy God'd Apostle, or that you should marry his widow after him at any time. Truly such a thing is in God's sight an enormity." (33:53)

Verse 33:53 was addressed to Muslim males of the Prophet's (pbuh) time, asking for specific behaviour towards the wives of the Prophet (pbuh). The expression 'ask for anything you want' refers to asking from the wives of the Prophet (pbuh) as is clear from the context at the beginning of 33:53.

- "Whether you reveal anything or conceal it, verily God has full knowledge of all things." (33:54)

- "There is no blame (on these ladies if they appear) before their fathers, or their sons, or their brothers, or their brother's sons, or their sister's sons, or their women, or the (slaves) whom their right hand posess. And (ladies) fear God, for God is Witness to all things." (33:55)

From the context of 33:53, the excluded persons from the rules of seclusion mentioned in 33:55 refer specifically to the Prophet's (pbuh) wives. In view of the abolition of slavery, the rules regarding seclusion from slaves are obsolete.

- "O Prophet! Tell your wives and daughters, and the believing women, that they should cast their outer garments (*jilbabs*) over their persons (when abroad): that is most convenient that they should be known (as such) and not molested. And God is Oft-Forgiving, Most Merciful." (33:59)

- "O you who believe! Enter not houses other than your own, until you have asked permission and saluted those in them: that is best for you, in order that you may heed (what is seemly).

  If you find no one in the house, enter not until permission is given to you: if you are asked to go back, go back: that makes for greater purity for yourselves: and God knows all that you do.

  It is no fault on your part to enter houses not used for living in, which serve some (other) use for you: and God has knowledge of what you reveal and what you conceal." (24:27–29)

- "O you who believe! Let those whom your right hand possesses, and the (children) among you who have not come of age, ask your permission (before they come to your presence), on three occassions: before morning prayer; the while you doff your clothes for the noon day heat; and after the late night prayer: these are your three times of undress. Outside these times it is not wrong for you or for them to move about attending to each other: thus God makes clear the Signs to you: for God is full of knowledge and wisdom.

  And when the children among you come of age, let them (also) ask for permission, as to those senior to them (in age): thus God makes clear His Signs to you: for God is full of knowledge and wisdom.

  And such elderly women as are past the prospect of marriage, —there is no blame on them if they lay aside their (outer) garments, provided they make not a wanton display of their beauty: but it is best for them to be modest: and God is one who sees and knows all things." (24:58–60)

(The rules regarding the slaves in 24:58 are obsolete in view of the abolition of slavery.)

- "It is no fault in the blind nor in one born lame, nor in one afflicted with illness, nor in yourselves, that you should eat in your own houses, or those of your father's, or your mother's, or your brother's, or your sister's, or your father's brothers, or your father's sisters, or your mother's brothers or your mother's sisters, or in houses of which the keys are in your possession, or in the house of a sincere friend of yours: there is no blame on you whether you eat in company or separately. But if you enter houses, salute each other—a greeting of blessing and purity as from God. Thus does God make clear the Signs to you that you may understand." (24:61)

From a careful analysis of the relevant Quranic verses dealing with seclusion, we can see some of the verses are addressed to Muslim women generally, and some refer to all Muslim women, including the Prophet's (pbuh) wives and his daughters (e.g. 33:59). The third category of verses from their context and the persons addressed therein are meant exclusively for the Prophet's (pbuh) wives. The greater restrictions and privacy imposed by these verses were not meant for ordinary Muslim women. These particular verses are 32, 33, 53, 54, and 55 of the thirty-third sura (chapter) of the Quran. In this context Leila Ahmed's (1992) remarks are very significant. According to Ahmed, all verses asking for the seclusion of women applied during the Prophet's (pbuh) lifetime to his wives only. She further suggests that the early texts about the background of the revelation of these verses used the expression '*hijab*,' meaning veil or seclusion, and the expression '*darabat al-hijab*' meaning, she took the veil, also meant she became the wife of the Prophet (pbuh). Again, *hijab* meant curtain, indicating partition or separation. Ahmed adds further that in those early days of Islamic history, the term *hijab* was used generally to refer to the seclusion of the Prophet's (pbuh) wives and to the orders relating to their veiling or covering their bodies. In the Hadith, using the expression 'she took the veil' meant the woman became the Prophet's (pbuh) wife and for sometime after the death of the Prophet (pbuh), when the materials of the Hadiths were circulated, veiling and seclusion were still considered peculiar to the Prophet's (pbuh) wives. Like others, Leila Ahmed is unsure how the custom of veiling became applicable to ordinary Muslim women. However, it can be presumed that the combined result of the custom of veiling prevailing among the non-Muslim in the conquered territories and the acceptance of the Prophet's (pbuh) wives as role models may have contributed to the general adoption of the custom of veiling among Muslim women.

While analyzing 24:30 and 24:31, we notice both men and women are asked to behave in the same manner and in the same words (i.e. 'lower their gaze and guard their modesty') and these particular portions of 24:30 and 24:31 presuppose that women will appear in public. However in 24:31, the expression, "*wa laa yubdiina ziinatahunna illamaa zahara minhaa*" meaning "And they should not display their beauty and ornaments except what appears thereof" applies exclusively to women. It is therefore important to find out exactly what is meant by *zinat*. Interpreting *zinat* as the beauty of the body, some Islamic jurists suggest the Islamic prohibition against the display of the beauty of women's bodies is total and there is no exception even to the limited, specified persons in the last part of this verse. It goes without saying these jurists were wrong in denying the display of women's beauty to these specified persons. Other groups of Islamic jurists, including Muhammad Ali (1951), on the strength of the clause in 24:31 which says, "and they should not strike their feet in order to draw attention to their hidden zinats" conclude that *zinat* consists of external ornaments or jewellery as those are the only things which can be known by striking the feet. Interpreting the expression in 24:31, "except what appears thereof" Muhammad Ali (1951) says it means 'except that which is customary or natural to uncover.' Hazrat Akram and Hazrat Dhahak have interpreted the same expression as the face, the hand, and the feet (up to the ankle). Tabari (1984) says the most correct opinion is that the exception relates to the face and the hands. However, according to Ibn Masud, Ibn Shirin, and Abul Jawza, the expression refers to the kind of beauty which depends on clothes, ornaments, et cetera which women should not deliberately display (Khan n.d.). Tabari (1984) summarizes the exceptions when Muslim women are not required to cover in the following manner: (a) they need not cover the adornments such as collyrium, rings, and bracelets (b) they need not cover the adornment of dress or clothes they wear (c) they need not cover their face and hands. at-Tabari adds further that while praying women are obliged to uncover their faces and half of their wrists, they are not required to keep their faces and hands (up to elbow) covered. Summarizing Muslim women's duties regarding the covering of their bodies, Asghar ali Engineer (1992) states the only Quranic requirement for them in this matter is not to display their sexual charms, and to have dignified dress.

The expression '*wal yazribna bi khumurihinna alaa juyuu bihinna*' meaning 'and they should draw their *khumar* over their bosoms' in 24:31 needs a careful analysis. Translating *khimar* (plural *khumar*) as 'head covering,' Muhammad Ali (1951) states the Quran asks Muslim women to use their head coverings to cover their breasts. Muhammad Ali (1950) also gives the historical background to this portion of 24:31. He informs us that women of pre-Islamic Arabia used to display their beauty by uncovering their breasts although they had their head coverings and the Quran reformed this bad practice by asking Muslim women to cover their bosoms by using their head coverings. Therefore the main emphasis of this portion of 24:31 is for covering the bosoms of Muslim women, their head coverings used in those days being the most suitable part of their dress or clothing to cover their bosoms. Thus, while covering the breasts is obligatory on a Muslim woman, the Quran did not ask them to cover their heads as well. According to a Hadith, the Prophet (pbuh) addressed Asma (Aisha's sister) when she appeared before the Prophet in thin clothes by the following words, "O Asma, when a woman attains her puberty, it is not proper that any part of her body should be seen except this," and he pointed to his face and hands (AD 31:30). This Hadith is found in Abu Daud's collection of Sahi Hadith and is reported by Khalid bin Darik. It is alleged to have been narrated by Aisha. This alleged Hadith is *mursal* (a weak Hadith) and a doubtful one, in view of the fact that there is no proof Khlaid bin Darik ever met Aisha. Even assuming this is an authentic Hadith, it asks women reaching puberty not to wear thin clothes, which reveal their bodily charms.

The expression, '*wa laa tabarrajna tabarrujal jahiliyyatil uulaa*' in 33:33 meaning 'and don't display your beauty like the displaying of the former times of ignorance' needs further attention. The term used in verse 33:33 of the Quran for displaying of beauty is '*tabarruj.*' Another derivative of '*tabarruj*' is '*burooj*' (used in the Quran in 4:77, 15:16, 25:61, and 85:1), which means 'tower' (because of their clear visibility). This verse is addressed to the Prophet's (pbuh) family. Those who argue 33:33 is also applicable to Muslim women generally suggest women are forbidden from using a dress, walking, or behaving in a manner which may result in clear visibility of their bodies. Whether 33:33 applies to the Prophet's (pbuh) family only, or to women generally, the Prophet's (pbuh) comment on the dresses of the women of Banu Tameem tribe visiting Aisha in thin clothes is noteworthy. On seeing them the Prophet (pbuh) said to these ladies, "If you are believers, then these are not believers' clothing" (Al-Qaradawi 1994).

The expression '*yudniina alayhinna min jalaabibihinna*' meaning 'that they should cast their outer garments (*jilbabs*) over their persons' in 33:59 is addressed to the wives and the daughters of the Prophet (pbuh) and to all believing women generally. Lane (1980) translates '*jilbab*' as a garment with which women cover their other garments, or a woman's head covering, or a garment with which she covers her head and bosom. Muhammad Ali (1950) thinks that *jilbab* may be part of an ordinary dress or may be a kind of overcoat. Discussing the background to the revelation of 33:59, Muhammad Ali (1951) states there was a reason for the free Muslim women of Medina to wear *jilbab*. Ali opines that it was to distinguish them from slaves, so that they were not molested by the hypocrites (as suggested in the last part of 33:60) and those in whose hearts is a disease (as mentioned in 33:60). Muhammad Ali (1950) comments that the use of *jilbab* is not compulsory under all circumstances but is a kind of protection when there is fear or trouble. The language used in 33:59 supports Muhammad Ali's comment as 33:59 does not order but recommends the use of *jilbab* by saying that 'they should cast their *jilbabs* over their persons.' Muhammad Asad (1984) agrees with Muhammad Ali's opinion on 33:59 and opines that the deliberate vagueness about the recommendation of *jilbab* makes it clear their use was not meant to be an injunction (*hukm*), but a moral guideline to be followed at a particular time or in a particular environment. According to Mohammad Asad, the reference to God's forgiveness and mercy in this verse strengthens this interpretation. According to Muhammad Ali (1951) the relaxation for older women to put off their clothes without making a wanton display of their beauty (in 24:60) refers to putting off *jilbab*.

Verse 7:26 of the Quran deals with the purpose of clothing which are stated as being (a) to guard against evil, (b) to cover shame, and (c) to increase beauty. Therefore, it is permissible for both men and women to enhance their beauty with clothing provided their shame is covered and they are guarded against evil. Verses 6:151 and 7:33 of the Quran forbid Muslim indecencies, whether open or secret, apparent or concealed. It is therefore clear, that what God expects from both male and female Muslims is not only to have proper dress and coverings, but also to have minds free from indecencies. This is the Islamic requirement in the relationship between men and women and between one Muslim and another.

Verses 24:27-29 lay down the rules a Muslim is required to follow while entering the houses of others. Verse 24:58–59 lay down rules of privacy for the adults from their underage children and from their slaves. According to these verses, children and slaves have to seek permission from their parents, guardians, and masters, respectively, before entering the rooms occupied by the parents, guardians, or masters on three specified occasions. These verses also lay down rules of privacy to be observed by adult children by seeking permission to enter the private place of their parent's or guardian's at all times of the day and night. The rules regarding slaves are obsolete because of the abolition of slavery.

Verse 24:61 of the Quran deals with eating with particular types of persons and the right manners when entering houses. The Quran justifies eating with blind, lame, or sick people against the stigma of eating with these persons in pre-Islamic Arabia. The other part of 24:61 justifies eating with close relatives. Commenting on 24:61, Muhammad Ali (1951) states that because of familiarities with near relatives, this verse recommends taking food with them, even if not specially invited.

So far we have based our discussion on the text of the Quran as interpreted by commentators with the help of authentic Hadith and in the context of the history of Muslims. However, we are aware the Quran has given us only the fundamentals of Islamic principles and the detailed rules on various matters are not always available within it. We are asked by Islamic principles to search for these rules in the Hadith or in the *Qiyas* (deduction on the basis of Quranic verses and the Hadith). This method of searching for answers was approved by the famous Hadith of the Prophet (pbuh) told to Muadh bin Jabal on the eve of his migration to Ethiopia, as the leader of a group of Muslims. Therefore, from now on attempts will be made to answer all relevant questions arising in the discussion of the present subject with the help of the Quran, the Hadith, and the *Qiyas* in light of the history of Muslims while not contradicting the principles laid down by the Quran at any stage.

The Quranic verses discussed above imply clearly that women are expected to come out of their houses if and when the necessity arises. The Hadith of the Prophet (pbuh) makes the position more clear. The Prophet (pbuh) said, "It is permitted to you (the women) to go out for your needs" (B 4:13, 67:116). Going out of the house obviously requires a woman to come into contact with men and intermingling of the two sexes cannot be avoided. This is precisely the reason why the Quran has laid down rules to be observed on such occasions. Therefore, the views of many Muslim conservatives that a woman's real place is at home has no support either in the Quran or the Hadith. In fact, Muslim women are in the same position as Muslim men who also come out of their houses only for their needs. The study of the Hadith and the history of Muslims show clearly the circumstances when Muslim women came out of their houses for their needs.

Regarding Muslim women leaving their houses for religious purposes, there are innumerable Hadiths and many historical instances to show women's participation in religious services in the mosques and other places. Following are some relevant Hadiths and historical facts relevant on this subject:

- The Prophet (pbuh) said, "Do not prohibit the handmaids of Allah from going to the mosques of Allah." (B 11:12)

- The Prophet (pbuh) said, "If a woman wanted to go to the mosque at night, she should not be prohibited from doing so." (B 10:162)

- The Prophet (pbuh) said, "When the wife of one of you asks permission to go out she should not be prohibited from doing so." (B 10:166)

- Atika Binte Zayed used to tell her husband, Hazrat Umar bin Khattab, "By Allah I shall pray in the mosque until you specifically forbid me to do so." But how could Umar forbid his wife to do so as he knew that the Prophet had said "Do not stop your wife from going to the mosque." (Abu Daud)

- On one night when the Prophet (pbuh) was very late in coming out to lead the Esha (night) prayers, the Prophet said, "Umar, call out: the women and the children are going to sleep."

- Hazrat Aisha said that women used to be present at the morning prayers, which was said at an hour so early that they returned to their houses while it was still dark. (B 8:13)

- Another Hadith mentions that the Prophet (pbuh) shortened his prayers when he heard a baby crying so that the mother of a suckling child should not be inconvenienced. (B 10:65)

- The women used to take part in the congregational prayers of Fajr, Maghrib and Esha and if they could finish their domestic work they also took part in the congregational prayers of Zuhr and Asar. (Bukhari, Muslim and Tirmidhi)

- The practice for women to be present in the mosques at the time of prayers seems to have continued long after the Prophet's time. Within the mosques they were not separated from men by any screen or curtain; only they formed into a line behind the men. (B 10:164)

- Though the women were covered decently with an over garment, they did not wear a veil. (Ali 1950)

- On the ocassion of the great gathering of the pilgrimage *(Hajj)* that is obligatory for both men and women, the women are expressly forbidden to wear a veil. (B 25:23)

- In the year 256 AH, the Governor of Mecca is said to have tied rope between the columns to make a separate place for women. Muhammad Ali (1950) comments, "Later on, the practice grew up of erecting a wooden barrier in the mosque to form a separate place for women, but by and by the purdah conception grew so strong that women were altogether shut out from the mosques."

- Regarding the *Jumma* prayer, the Prophet (pbuh) said, "The *Jumma* prayer is obligatory to everybody except the sick, the women, the children and the slaves. However there is no bar against the women regarding their attendance at *Jumma* prayer, rather their attendance at Jumma prayer will entitle them to rewards from Allah." (Abu Daud)

- Hazrat Umme Atiya said, "Although we (the women) were asked not to participate in the *Janaza* prayer (service for the dead), our (women's) attendance was not forbidden. Once Hazrat Umar criticized a woman for being present at the *Janaza* prayer and hearing that, the Prophet (pbuh) said "O Umar, don't annoy her." (Ibn Maja, Nesai)

- Regarding *Eed* prayers, Asim bin Sulaiman said that Hafsa Binte Shirin had said that, "We have been ordered (by the Prophet) to come out on the *Eed* day with our unmarried daughter and even with women who had started their menstruation. On the *Eed* day the women will stand behind the men, will utter the *takbir*, will participate in the prayer and will pray for the sanctity and happiness of the *Eed* day." (Bukhari)

- Hazrat Abbas has said that, "The Prophet (pbuh) used to participate at the *Eed* prayers with his wives and daughters. (Ibne Maja)

- In the mosques the women were not forbidden to speak to the men. Once Hazrat Ayesha could not hear the last part of the sermon of the Prophet (pbuh) as his companions (*ahsabs*) were crying loudly and then she had asked a man sitting by her side and said, "May God be kind to you. Could you tell me what were the last words of the Prophet?" The man said that the Prophet (pbuh) had said, "It has been revealed to me that you have to face the test of the grave before the test of your *dajjal.*" (Nesai)

It is clear from the above that women are allowed to go to the mosque and the only prescribed rule for their position in the congregational prayer is to be in a line behind the men. There is no obligation for them to wear a veil. It is therefore obvious the two sexes have to intermingle in the same room or in the same yard in the mosque. In the pilgrimage *(Hajj)*, there is much greater intermingling of the sexes, women performing circumambulation of the *Kaba*, running between *Safa* and *Marwa*, staying in the plain of Arafat and going from place to place without a veil, side by side with men. Tabari (1967–69) says, "Until the 3rd century A. H.

and even later, women used to pray in mosques, along with men. They were not required to be veiled. However, the law books prescribed that dress to be worn should be in two pieces. The face, hands and upper side of the feet need not be covered, though there is some controversy about the last detail."

Ibne Batuta (1958) says, "Their (the Muslim's) women showed no modesty in the presence of men and did not veil. Yet they were assiduous in their prayers . . . the women there have friends and companions amongst men who are not related to them. So also the men have friends amongst women who are not related to them. A man may enter his house and find his wife with her friend and yet will not disapprove."

A woman's right to choose her husband presupposes the woman has found out all the information about her prospective husband and has also seen him if she thinks it is necessary. The Quran says, "When you divorce women, and they fulfill the terms of their *(iddat),* do not prevent them from marrying their husbands if they mutually agree on equitable terms . . . " (2:232). The Prophet (pbuh) said, "When one of you makes a proposal of marriage to a woman, then if he can, he should look at what attracts him to marry her" (AD 12:18). Imam Bukhari's collection of Hadith has a chapter with a heading, "To look at the woman before marriage" (B 67:36). Imam Muslim's collection of Hadith has a chapter with a heading, "Inviting a man who intends to marry a woman to have a look at her face and hands" (M 16:12). Mughira Ibn Shuba, a companion of the Prophet (pbuh), made a proposal of marriage to a woman and was asked by the Prophet (pbuh) to see her as "it was likely to bring about greater love and concord between them" (M 13:2–11). Since Islamic marriage is a contract affected by the consent of both the parties, and particularly in view of Quranic verse 2:232, it would seem the woman has the same right to satisfy herself about her future husband by looking at him and finding out all the necessary information about him before giving her consent. Ahmad Shukri (n.d.), quoting Abdul Qadir says, "The time for seeing should precede the betrothal. The woman is recommended to have a look at the man if she wants to marry him; because anything that would please her with him will please him with her . . . and each of them can renew his or her glances whenever he or she wants, in order to discuss the features of his or her object, so that he or she may not repent after marriage." Nowadays when women and men are coming into contact with each other on countless occasions in their day to day lives and having conversations with each other on various subjects, it is totally unreasonable to suppose the rights of the prospective partners of marriage cease at just seeing each other. It is essential that the prospective partners should have conversations regarding each other's likes and dislikes, choices and preferences, and interests and disinterests, as there is no specific prohibition against such conversations between the prospective husband and wife. Hafiz Sheikh Ahmed (133 AH) in his *Nurul Anwar* has observed, "Lawfulness is a recognized principle in all things." Explaining this principle, Muhammad Ali (1950) states that unless it is definitely prohibited by Islamic law, everything and every free act of a person is presumed to be lawful. This dictum is in fact based on the words of the Quran, "He it is who created for you all that is in the earth" (2:29). Conservative Muslim jurists, while imposing restrictions on women, reserve the prospective husband's rights to see the faces of their future brides before making a proposal of marriage. All four Sunni schools of law permit suitor to look at the face and hands of the bride before deciding to marry her. Hanafis permit the inspection of her legs. Daud al-Zahiri (founder of Zahiri School) gave the suitor the right to look at the whole body of the girl, except her private parts, before his final decision to marry her. It is regrettable these jurists denied similar rights to the prospective wife; the only right she had was to cast a fleeting glance towards her prospective husband. Even a close look at him was condemned as an act of immodesty (Lokhandwala 1987).

Looking at rules of social interaction, there is no bar against intermingling of people of opposite sexes in social functions. We have records of three occasions from history as examples of intermingling for social functions.

1. Imam Bukhari has informed us about a bride serving the male guests of her husband in the marriage feast. (Walima)

2. On the seventh *Hijri* an Abyssinian (Ethiopian) delegation came to Medina. A group of gymnasts among the delegation performed their gymnastics inside the mosque of Medina. The Prophet (pbuh) enjoyed their performance along with Hazrat Ayesha. (Bukhari, Muslim, Nesai, Musnad of Imam Ahmed bin Hanbal)

3. The musical functions arranged by Hazrat Syeda Sakina Binte Hussain were attended by many influential people of Medina. Syed Ameer Ali has mentioned many such social functions organized by Hazrat Sakina and by Ayesha Binte Talha on the authority of Kitabul Aghani by Abul Faraj al-Ispahani. (1963)

Regarding the participation of Muslim men and women in intellectual, religious, and spiritual pursuits, we have innumerable instances of talented and educated Muslim women making brilliant contributions. At least a few of these women deserve special mention. Hazrat Ayesha was one of the greatest and most reliable of the narrators of Hadith. The *Sihah Sitta* contains 2210 Hadith narrated by her. She regularly addressed the companions of the Prophet (pbuh) on religious topics and specifically Hadith. Hazrat Syeda Zainab Binte Ali and Hazrat Syeda Sakina Binte Hussain Ibne Ali were brilliant orators who gave lectures on religion and social problems. Syeda Sakina was also a famous poet. Malik Binte Sharif, Fatima Binte Abbas, Fatima Binte Shehal Ahmed, Fatima Binte Jalaluddin, Fatima Binte Ibrahim Mukaddasi, Fatima Binte Syed Ahmed, and Fatima Binte Takiuddin were famous speakers on Islam whose speeches from the *mimbar* of the mosques and other places earned them great fame. In the field of mysticism (*tasawwaf*) the fame and universal recognition of the following women were beyond dispute: Hazrat Hafsa, Hazrat Fakhira Binte Usman, Syeda Nafisa Binte Hussain Ibne Ali, Sayrana, Khadiza, Rabeya Jilani, and Rabeya Al Basari. The great Sufi, Hasan al-Basari used to solve his questions on mysticism through his discussion with Hazrat Rabeya al-Basari. Similarly Hazrat Bayezid Bustami used to admit that only Hazrat Fatima Nishapuri could give satisfactory answers to his questions on mysticism.

Regarding Muslim women's participation in warfare and related activities, no purdah or seclusion could stand in the way of Muslim women taking an active part on the battlefields in various capacities. The cause of Islam was as important to women as it was to men. Even members of the Prophet's (pbuh) family and his closest relations were not hesitant to come out of their home to fight in the defense of Islam. On the critical battlefield of Uhad, Hazrat Ayesha and Umme Salama exhausted themselves in running to supply water to the thirsty soldiers. In this battle, Hazrat Umme Aammir suffered several injuries while acting as a shield to protect the Prophet (pbuh). Rabi Binte Muaz and other women carried injured and martyred Muslim soldiers from the battlefield of Uhad. Muslim women carried out similar roles on the battlefield of Kadesiya. Hazrat Sufiya, a paternal aunt of the Prophet (pbuh), was engaged in defending a Muslim camp in a battle. Hazrat Asma Binte Abu Bakr took an active part in many battles including the battle of Yarmuk along with her husband. Hazrat Juwoayriah, the sister of Hazrat Muwayiah, led a division of Muslim women soldiers at the battle of Yarmuk; prominent roles were also played by Khawla Binte Khalba, Kanab Binte Malik, Salma Binte Hashim, Naam Binte Kanas, Afira Binte Afara, and Umme Hakim.

Muslim women showed extraordinary heroism at the battle of Aznavain under the leadership of Khawla Binte Azda, Afra Binte Iffara, and Umme Abu Salma. Hazrat Sumayya, the mother of the Sahaba Hazrat Ammar, was the first martyr of Islam who died saving the life of the Prophet (pbuh). Hazrat Sumayya was killed by Abu Jahal. Long before Florence Nightingale organized her nurses to serve the soldiers in the Crimea, Hazrat Ummiah Gifari organized Muslim women with great efficiency and scientific precision to form a cadre of nurses to serve the Muslim soldiers on the battlefield.

While Islam has always encouraged the mixing of the opposite sexes whenever necessity demanded it, Islam has also discouraged unnecessary mingling of the sexes or the mixing of persons of opposite sexes in compromising circumstances. However, Islam has never prohibited women from being alone with men who are their '*dhu mahram*' (persons with whom marriage is prohibited). Muslim women have been prohibited from being alone in private with a man who is not her '*dhu mahram*' (B 67:112). But when other people are present or the woman is exposed to public view, there is no harm for a woman to be alone with men who are not her *dhu mahram* (B 67:113). Imam Shafii justified the *mahram* rule for traveling Muslim woman for her protection, security, and to preserve her chastity. However, as we have found in our discussion above, the *mahram* rule, if at all relevant in the difficult circumstances of the male dominated Arab society of the Middle Ages, is not at all obligatory on modern Muslim women. This rule is definitely inapplicable to Muslim women performing the Hajj among a large number of men and women.

In view of our above discussion we come to the conclusion that Islam has never asked for the unnatural barrier between men and women as we find in the modern purdah system. The spirit of purdah the Quran and the Hadith prescribe is the sense of chastity and decorum that can restrain the sexual passions of men and women, and can prevent indecencies. We do not know what methods modern Islamic society will adopt to reform the prevailing purdah system, but it can be said with certainty that Muslim women are not subject to any authority other than the Quran and only those authentic Hadith which are not contradictory to the letter and spirit of the Quran. Muslim women are free to transact the business and occupations of modern life as much as their male counterparts, provided they remain within the limits of Islam. The problems they might confront and what solutions they must arrive at in this supreme challenge to all the reactionary restrictions and taboos accumulated during the last one thousand years, is for Muslim women to decide. Is it not time for them to say that enough is enough? The Muslim world is waiting impatiently for the day when liberated Muslim women will be free to contribute their best towards the political, social, economic, moral, and intellectual development of their community along with Muslim men. We hope that day is not far off.

12

Women in Politics
and as the Head of a State

Women's rights to participate in politics and to become a head of state or that of an administration has been challenged by conservative theologians as being un-Islamic. In the following discussion their opinion on this matter has been considered and rejected. As more and more Muslim women exercise their legitimate rights in different spheres of life it is quite natural that they will aspire to assume positions of authority in government. A clash has existed throughout Islamic history between conservatives who have aimed to restrict a Muslim woman's ability to lead a political life and liberals who have sought to allow a Muslim woman's legitimate right to sit in a position of authority. Let us explore what the original sources say on this matter.

The Quran is silent about the specific question as to whether or not a woman can become the head of a Muslim state. However, the Quran does not deny women the privilege of leading a political life or of heading a Muslim state. In fact, many verses of the Quran, exemplified by the verses quoted in the first two pages of chapter 2 of this book, clearly mention that women have been given absolute equality with men so far as reward and punishment for their deeds by God are concerned. These verses are 5:10–11, 5:72, 4:125, 32:19–20, 45:22, 49:13, 3:195, 4:124, 33:35, 40:40, and 49:11 of the Quran.

Two of the finest and respected translators of the Quran support the above view about women. Thus, Abdullah Yusuf Ali (1946) commenting on 3:195 states categorically that the Quran not only recognizes the equal

121

status of the sexes but also insists on this status for women. Similarly, Muhammad Ali (1951) states that by repeating ten times that women can attain every good quality men have access to in 33:35, the Quran asserts that women can obtain the same spiritual level as men.

Turning to the question of women as heads of state, some very significant verses of the Quran deal with the Queen of Sheba as head of state with approval from the chiefs. Following are these relevant Quranic verses.

- "She said, 'You chiefs! Advise me in (this) my affair: no affair have I decided except in your presence.'

- They said, 'We are endued with strength, and given to vehement war: but the command is with you; so consider what you will command.'

- She said, 'Kings, when they enter a country, despoil it, and make the noblest of its people its meanest. Thus, do they behave. But I am going to send him a present, and (wait) to see with what (answers) return (my) ambassadors'" (27:32–35).

These verses of the Quran clearly show the Queen of Sheba was the legitimate ruler of her people who made wise decisions independent of the advice of her chiefs or advisers, and that they clearly approved of her decisions. Nowhere in these verses is there an indication that the Quran disapproves of her rule as head of state. In fact, in further verses of the Quran (27:43–44), a description is given of her submission to Islam, again independent of chiefs or advisors. The verses 27:43 and 27:44 are as follows:

- "And he (Solomon) diverted her (Queen of Sheba) from the worship of others besides God: for she was (sprung) of a people that had no faith" (27:43).

- " . . . She (Queen of Sheba) said: 'O my Lord! I have indeed wronged my soul: I do (now) submit (in Islam) with Solomon to the Lord of the worlds'" (27:44).

Let us now turn to one specific, alleged saying of the Prophet (pbuh) which the anti-women conservatives in Muslim society have advanced as their argument for excluding women from the position of head of state. In this Hadith, reported by Abu Bakra, the Prophet (pbuh) is alleged to have opposed a woman having the right to be head of state. The specific Hadith is an '*ahad Hadith*,' meaning it is an isolated Hadith that was not reported by more than one of the companions of the Prophet (pbuh). During the election campaign of Fatima Jinnah for the presidency of Pakistan in 1962, and during the campaign of Benazir Bhutto in the general election of Pakistan in 1988, the anti-woman faction of Pakistan used this particular Hadith as the basis of their opposition to a woman's right to become the president or prime minister of Pakistan. Following are the two versions of the alleged Hadith as reported by Abu Bakra.

- "Those who entrust their affairs to women will never have prosperity" (Bukhari 1973).

- "That nation can never prosper which has assigned its reign to a woman" (Bukhari 1973).

It is essential to explore the historical background to this alleged saying of the Prophet (pbuh). The famous historian al-Asqalani (1982) gives us the background of this alleged Hadith. Al-Asqalani tells us that when the Prophet (pbuh) was told that the daughter of Kisra (King of Persia) had succeeded her dead father, the Prophet (pbuh) is supposed to have said the above Hadith. From our study of Persian history between 628 and 632 A.D. we learn that during the unstable political situation of Persia after the assassination of the Persian King Khusraw Pavis, two women emerged as claimants to the Sassanid throne. It is quite possible that on the ascension to the throne by one of these two women claimants, the Prophet (pbuh) might have said the above Hadith reported by Abu Bakra. It is noticeable that Abu Bakra is the only companion of the Prophet (pbuh) who heard this Hadith and he is the only one to report it. Therefore, even if we accept this Hadith solely reported by Abu Bakra as a genuine one, it is quite possible this alleged comment of the Prophet (pbuh) was confined to the isolated instance of the troubled situation of Persia. Tabari (n.d.), the famous historian and *mufassir* tells us Abu Bakra informed us about this particular Hadith when Hazrat Ayesha besieged Basra (where Abu Bakra was living) and was asked for the support of the notables of the city in her (alleged) rightful cause against Caliph Ali. Many of the inhabitants and the *Sahabas* of the Prophet (pbuh), including the governor, Abu Musa-al-Ashari, remained neutral (in this conflict between Ali and Ayesha) on the basis of opposing *fitna* (civil war). At the assembly of the citizens of Kufa, in the central Mosque of Kufa, Abu Musa spoke against joining any side as it would be *fitna* and he quoted many Hadiths against *fitna*. The only person (among the *Sahabas*) who opposed supporting Hazrat Ayesha because she was a woman, and the

Prophet (pbuh) had forbidden entrusting power to a woman was Abu Bakra. He claimed that he told Ayesha his reason (i.e. the Prophet's (pbuh) alleged Hadith against women) for not joining her cause. However, public knowledge about Abu Bakra's reason for not supporting Ayesha was his opposition to *fitna*. It is interesting to note Abu Musa al-Ashari was dismissed by Caliph Ali from the position of Governor for not supporting Ali but no harm came to Abu Bakra despite his neutrality. Bakra was allowed to take advantage of the general amnesty offered by Caliph Ali. Mernissi (1991) questions the coincidence of Abu Bakra remembering this particular Hadith twenty-five years after the Prophet (pbuh) was alleged to have said it, and at a time when Hazrat Ayesha (a woman) was utterly defeated by Caliph Ali at the Battle of the Camel.

Abu Bakra also heard another convenient Hadith (at a convenient moment) when Hasan-b-Ali gave up his right to the Caliphate to Muawiya when he (Muawiya) badly needed Hasan's support for his claim to the Caliphate. This time, Abu Bakra remembered that he heard the Prophet (pbuh) say, "Hasan (the son of Ali) will be the man of reconciliation" (al-Asqalani 1982). Once again, Abu Bakra remained on the winning side as Muawiyah was then firmly in power as Caliph of the Muslims.

Before considering Abu Bakra's reported Hadith about the disqualification of women for the position of head of state, we must note the fundamental test for accepting a Hadith as genuine. Dr. Abdul Hamid Mutawalli (n.d.) opines that a Hadith is not acceptable as genuine if it fails either of the following three tests:

1. A Hadith which is in conflict with the Quran.

2. A Hadith that contradicts the facts of history.

3. A Hadith that describes something which is impossible to believe.

From the study of the Quran, it is quite clear this particular Hadith, narrated by Abu Bakra, is in conflict with the Quranic verses quoted earlier (27:32–35 and 33:35). On this basis alone the alleged Hadith cannot be accepted as genuine. Imam Malik (1981) also describes means of testing an alleged saying of the Prophet (pbuh) for authenticity. The alleged Hadith about women narrated by Abu Bakra, fails the first test of Imam Malik as Abu Bakra was neither a jurist nor a political scientist well-versed in constitutional law. Abu Bakra, also failed the second test of Imam Malik because Bakra was presumed to be lying about his relationships with other people even though he was not found to be lying about religion. Abu Bakra's failure to satisfy the second test of Imam Malik was established when Abu Bakra was not believed as a witness to the alleged fornication by al-Mughira Ibn Shuba. Abu Bakra's cowitness to the same incident admitted that he was not really sure he saw everything. For his failure to be accepted as a truthful witness to the alleged fornication by al-Mughira, Caliph Umar I punished Abu Bakra by flogging due to his slander (al-Athir n.d.).

Despite the fact this alleged Hadith (narrated by Abu Bakra) is included in the *Sahih Bukhari*, many *fuqahas* (jurists of Islamic law) have contested this Hadith and do not agree on the weight to be given to this alleged Hadith. Tabari, a famous historian and interpretor of the Quran, did not consider this alleged Hadith as sufficient basis for denying women the right of decision making and the right of participating in politics (al-Asqalani 1982). Justice Aftab Hussain (1987) questions the decisions of Pakistani theologians (*ulemas*) to deny women the right to be a head of state on the basis of this *ahad* Hadith. Maulana Umar Ahmed Usmani (1980) rejects this reported Hadith as forged since Abu Bakra did not remember it until the time of the Battle of Camel, long after it was alleged to have been said. Professor Abdul Hamid Mutawalli (n.d.) opines the Prophet's (pbuh) *ahkam* (ruling) regarding *imamah* (leadership) of the community of Muslims and their general governance cannot be applied for framing general law (*tashriam*) as the ruling relating to *imamah* was meant for a particular time and issued in accordance with the prevailing situation. All the constitutional matters are in the *imamah* category. Professor Mutawalli also states that Imam Abu Hanifa, founder of the Hanafi School of law, never accepted any *ahad* Hadith such as the alleged Hadith reported by Abu Bakra. Ashraf Ali Thanavi (n.d.), who accepts this alleged Hadith as genuine, opines that this particular Hadith refers to the first category of government (personalized rule) headed or ruled by a woman. He adds that "the reason for pronouncement for this tradition is that the people of Iran made the daughter of Khusraw Pavis their ruler." Professor Mutawalli summarizes the opinion of Maulana Thanavi regarding the rule of the Queen of Sheba. He states that, according to Maulana Thanavi, the rule by the Queen of Sheba was a consultative rule and thus removed the reason of nonwelfare resulting from a woman's rule and therefore, a woman as head of the state in a consultative rule can be allowed."

Although in a minority, a section of Muslim theologians have always supported a woman's right to become the head of state (Usmani 1980). History has also shown many examples of Muslim women assuming positions of leadership. Hazrat Ayesha's leadership of the opposition against

Hazrat Ali and leading so many eminent *sahabas* belies the theory that a woman cannot be the head of state or lead Muslims. Ayesha is not the only example of a female Muslim leader. There are several examples of Muslim women as leaders of states, provinces, and sects during several centuries of Muslim history. In the Indian subcontinent, we have seen many women become leaders of Muslim states, they include: Raziya Sultana, Chand Sultana, and Malika Nurjahan (coruler with Moghul Emperor Jehangir). During the late fifteenth century A.D. (early sixth century *hijra* era), Hurrah Malika Arwa Binte Ahmed headed the administration of the province of Yemen under the Fatimid Caliphs Mustansir, Moost'Ali, and Amir. She was also the '*Hujjah*' (the highest religious officer) under Caliph Amir. After the assassination of Caliph Amir, she became the ruler of Yemen having received the Fatimid mission (D'awah). The Kharijites of the Berber territory of North Africa had Layla as their leader. During the time of the Abbaside Caliphate, Zubeida (wife of Harun), Buran (wife of Mamun), and al-Khayzuran (wife of al-Mahdi) exercised great influence in the affairs of the state during the Caliphates of their respective husbands. Ulayyah, the daughter of al-Mahdi was also a woman of great influence (Hittie 1967).

It is most unfortunate that a section of Muslim society believes a woman cannot partake in politics and cannot become a head of state. The alleged saying of the Prophet (pbuh) this belief is based on has to be rejected for the reasons described in the above discussion. The spirit and word of the Quran does not prevent women from aspiring to leadership. Society in general, and Muslim women in particular, deserve to be aware of this so Muslim women throughout the world can make a full contribution to society at all levels. In the late twentieth century, four prominent women politicians, namely Benazir Bhutto in Pakistan, Khaleda Zia and Hasina Wajed in Bangladesh, and Sukornoputri in Indonesia have been elected to the positions of prime minister or president. Perhaps this sets a final seal on this argument and confirms that Muslim women can become heads of administrations in states with an absolute majority of Muslims and without any opposition from the Muslim theologians of these states.

References

Abduh, Muhammad. n.d. *Manar*. Vol. 4. Paris: J. Jomier, Le Commentaries Carnique du Manar.

Abu-Daud. n.d. *Sunan—Collection of Hadiths*. Kanpur: Mataba Majidi.

Ahmed, Hafiz Sheikh. 133 A.H. *Nurul Anwar*. Cairo: Mustafa al Babi al-Halabi.

Ahmed, Leila. 1992. *Women and Gender in Islam*. New Haven: Yale University Press.

Ahmed, Moulavi. n.d. Maintenance for the divorce. Kerala: n.p.

AIR: *All India Report*.

Ali, Abdullah Yusuf. 1946. *The Holy Quran—Text, translation and commentary*. Jeddah: Islamic Education Center Publications.

Ali, Jawwad. 1968–71. *Al-Mufassal Fi Tarikh Al-Arab Qabl Al-Islam*. Beirut: n.p.

Ali, Maulana Muhammad. n.d. *A Manual of Hadith*. Lahore: Ahmadiyyah Anjuman Ishaat Islam.

Ali, Maulana Muhammad. 1951. *The Holy Quran—Arabic text, translation, and commentary*. 4th ed. Lahore: Ahmadiyyah Anjuman Ishaat Islam.

Ali, Maulana Muhammad. 1950. *The religion of Islam—A comprehensive discussion of the sources, principles, and practices of Islam*. Lahore: Ahmadiyyah Anjuman Ishaat Islam.

Ali, Mir Ahmed. 1988. *The Holy Quran with English translation of the Arabic text and commentary according to the version of the Holy Ahlul-Bait*. New York: Tahrike Tarsile Quran.

Ali, Sayyid Ameer. 1976. *Mohammadan law*. Lahore: Law Publishing Co.

Ali, Syed Ameer. n.d. *A short history of the Saracens*. Karachi: National Book Foundation.

Anderson, J. N. D. and N. J. Coulson. n.d. *Islamic law in contemporary cultural change*. Unpublished manuscript.

al-Aqqad, Abbas Mahmud. 1959. *Women in the Quran*. Cairo: Darul Halal.

Asad, Muhammad. 1984. *The message of the Quran—Translated and explained*. Gibraltar: Dar al-Andulas Ltd.

al-Asqalani, Imam Hajar. 1982. *Bulugh Al-Maram min Adillah Al-Ahkam*. Benares: n.p.

al-Asqalani, Imam Hajar. 1301 A.H. *Fath-Al-Bari*. Cairo: Al-Matbaa Al-Bhiya Al-Misrya.

al-Athir, Ibn. n.d. *Usd Al-Ghaba Fi Tamyiz Al-Sahaba.*Vol. 5. Beirut: Dar Al-Fikr.

Azad, Maulana Abul Kalam. 1980. *Tarjuman Al-Quran.* Delhi: Kitab Bhavan.

Baihaqi, Abu Bakr Ahmad ibn al Husayn. n.d. *Sunaw Al Kubra.* 8 vols. Hyderabad: n.p.

Baillie, Neil. 1875. *Digest of Moohummuddun law: Part 1—Hanafi Law. 2ⁿᵈ rev. ed.* London: n.p.

al-Barr, Ibn Abd. n.d. *Al Intiqa Fi Fadl Al-Thalath Al-Aimma Al-Fuqaha.* Beirut: Dar Al-Kutub Al-Ilmiya.

Bukhari, Muhammad bin Ismail. 1973. *Sahih Al-Bukhari.* Translated from the Arabic into English with Arabic text by Muhammad Mohsin Khan. Medina: Dar Al-Arabia Publishing, Printing and Distribution.

Burton, John. 1994. *An introduction to the Hadith.* Edinburgh: Edinburgh University Press.

Coulson, N. J. 1964. *History of Islamic law.* Edinburgh: Edinburgh University Press.

Cowan, Milton. 1976. *A dictionary of modern written Arabic.* 3ʳᵈ ed. New York: ITACA New York Spoken Language Services.

Dahlavi, Shah Abdul Aziz. n.d. *Ujala Nafia.* Delhi: n.p.

Ejayz, Abu. n.d. *Al-Qawanin. N.P. n. p.*

Engineer, Asghar Ali. 1992. *The rights of women in Islam.* London: C. Hurst and Co.

Fida, Abul. 1325 A.H. *Al-Mukhtasar Fi Akhbar Al-Basaar.* Cairo: n. p.

Fyzee, Asaf. 1964. *Outlines of Muhammadan law.* London: Oxford University Press.

Goldziher, Ignaz. 1971. *Muslim studies.* London: Allen and Unwin.

Guillaume, Alfred. 1954. *Islam.* London: Penguin Books.

Hajar, Ibne. n.d. *Nuzhat An-Nazar.* N.p. n.p.

Hanbal, Ahmed. 1306 A.H. *Musnad of Imam Hanbal.* Cairo: Al-Maimuna Press.

al-Hibri, Azizah. 1982. *Women's Studies International Forum* 5:207–19. *A Study of Islamic herstory: how did we ever get into this mess?*

Hidayatullah, Arshad. 1977. *Mulla's principles of Mohammedan law.* 18ᵗʰ ed. Bombay: N. M. Tripathi Private Ltd.

Hittie, P. K. 1967. *History of the Arabs.* New York: St. Martin's Press.

Hussain, Aftab. 1987. *Status of women in Islam.* Lahore: n.p.

Ibn Batuta. 1958. *Voyages.* Cambridge: Cambridge University Press.

Ibn Hanbal, Imam Ahmad Ibn Muhammad. 1306 A.H. *Musnad.* Cairo: Al-Maimuna Press.

Ibn Maja, Abu Abdallah Muhammad Ibn Yazid. n.d. *Sunan.* Delhi: Mujtabi Press.

al-Ispahani, Abul Faraj. 1963. *Qitabul Aghani.* Beirut: Tarihya Al-Turath Al-Arabi.

Jassas, Imam Abu Bakr. 1347 A.H. *Ahkam Al-Quran.* Cairo: n.p.

Kathir, Ibne. 1966. *Al Bidayah Wa Al-Nihayah.* Vol. 2. Beirut: n.p.

Khan, Waihiduddin. n.d. *Women in Islamic Shariah.* N.p. n.p.

Lane, Edward. 1980. *An Arabic English Lexicon*. London: Librarie Dulibon.

Levy, Reuben. 1962. *social structure of Islam*. Cambridge: Cambridge University Press.

Lokhandwala, S. T. 1987. *Position of women under Islam*. Delhi: n.p.

Maqdisi, Allama. n.d. *Kitabul Mughni*. N.p. n.p.

Malik, Ibne-Anas. 1981. *Muwatta* Translated by Muhammad Rahimuddin. New Delhi: Mujtabi Press.

al-Marghinani, Abul Hasan Ali Ibn Abu Bakr. 1982. *The Hedaya or Guide—A commentary on the Mussulman Laws*. Translated by Charles Hamilton. Delhi: Islamic Book Trust.

Maudoodi, Maulana Abul Aala. 1987. *The laws of marriage and divorce in Islam*. Kuwait: Islamic Book Publishers.

Maudoodi, Maulana Abul Aala. 1983. *Tafsire Quran*. Lahore: Pakistan Islamic Publications Ltd.

Maudoodi, Maulana Abul Aala. 1958. *Tahfimul Quran—A translation and tafsir of the Quran in Urdu*. Translated into Bengali by Mohammad Abdul Rahim. Dhaka: Kausar Publications.

Mernissi, Fatima. 1991. *Women in Islam—A historical and theological inquiry*. Translated by Mary Jo Lakeland. Oxford: Basil Blackwell Ltd.

Muhsin, Amina Wadud. 1992. *Quran and women*. Kuala Lampur: Penerbit Fajar Bakti SDN BHD.

Mulki, Maulana Tahir. 1981. *Introduction to Rajam Asl Hadhay Ya Tazir*. Karachi: n.p.

Mulla. n.d. *Principles of Mohammedan Law*. 18th ed. Delhi: Tripathi Private Ltd.

Murtada, Mahibad Din Abul Faid. n.d. *Tajul Arus (a dictionary)*. N.p. n.p.

Muslim, Imam. n.d. *Kitab As-Sahih or Sahih Muslim*. N.p. n.p.

Mutawalli, Abdul Hamid. n.d. *Mabadi Nizam Al-Hukum Al-Islami*. Cairo: n.p.

al-Nesai, Abu Abd-ar-Rahman Ahmad Ibn Ali. 1335–37 a.h. Delhi: Mujtabi Press.

Nujaym, Allama Ibn. n.d. *Al-Bahr Al-Raiq*. N.p. n.p.

Numani, Shibli. 1987. *Sirah Al-Numan*. Delhi: n.p.

Parvez. 1979. *Matalib Al-Furqan*. Lahore. n.p.

Pickthall, Muhammad Marmaduke. 1977. *The glorious Quran—Text and explanatory translation*. New York: Muslim World League.

PLD: *Pakistan Legal Decisions*.

al-Qaradawi, Yusuf. 1994. *The lawful and prohibited in Islam*. Plainsfield: Ind. American Trust Publication.

Qayyim, Ibn. n.d. *Ilam Al-Muwaqqa*. Lahore: n.p.

Qutb, Saiyyid. 1980. *Fi Zilal Al-Quran*. Cairo: Dar al-Shuruq.

Raghib, Imam Abul Qasim. 1485. *Al-Mufradat fi Gharib Al-Quran*. Tiras: n.p.

Rahim, Sir Abdur. n.d. *Principles of Muhammadan jurisprudence*. London: Luzac and Co.

Rahman, Fazlur. 1980. *Major themes in the Quran*. Minneapolis, Minn.: Bibliotheca Islamica.

Rahman, Tanzilur. 1985. *Majmua-e-Qawanin-e-Islami*. Islamabad: Marqizi Idara-yi Tahqiqat Islami.

Razi, Fakhraddin. n.d. *Al-Tafsiral-Kabir (commentary)*. Beirut: Dar al Fikr.

Sa'd, Ibn. n.d. *Kitab Al-Tabaqat Al-Kabir*. Karachi: Pakistan Historical Society.

Schacht, Joseph. 1950. *The origin of Muhammadan jurisprudence*. Oxford: Clarendon Press.

Shafii, Muhammad bin Idris. n.d. *Kitab Al-Umm*. Cairo: n.p.

Shafii, Muhammad bin Idris. 1987. *Risala*. Translated from the Arabic into English by Majid Khudduri. Cambridge: n.p.

Shihab, Rafiullah. 1986. *Islamic Shariat and the Shah Bano case*. Lahore: Pakistan Times.

Shukri, Ahmed. n.d. *The Muhammadan law of marriage and divorce*. N.p. n.p.

Stowasser, Barbara Fryer. 1994. *Women in the Quran, traditions, and interpretations*. New York: Oxford University Press.

Sulaiman, Muhammad. 1935. *Purdah*. Calcutta: Book Tower.

Tabari, Muhammad bin Jarir. 1967–69. *Tarikh Al-Umami Wal-Muluk*. Cairo: Al-Hussainiyah Press.

Tabari, Muhammad bin Jarir. 1984. *Tafsir Jamial Bayan An-Tawil Ayi Al-Quran*. Beirut: Dar al-Fiqr.

Tabari, Muhammad bin Jarir. 1979. *Tarikh Al-Rasul Wal-Muluk*. Beirut: Dar Al-Fiqr.

Tabrizi, Shaikh Wahiduddin Abdullah. 1973. *Mishkatul Masabih*. Translated from Arabic into English by James Robson. Lahore: n.p.

Travis, Carol, and Carole Wade. 1984. *The longest war: Sex difference in perspective*. Orlando, Fla.: Harcourt Brace Jovanovich.

Taymiyah, Imam Ibn. n.d. *Al-Ikhtiyarat Al-Ilmiyiah*. Egypt: n.p.

Thanavi, Ashraf Ali. n.d. *Imad Al-Fatwa*. Karangi: Dar Ulm.

Tirmidhi, Abu Isa Muhammad Ibn Isa. 1895. *Al-Jami: Collection of Hadith*. Cairo: Bulaq.

Tyabji, Faiz Badruddin. 1940. *Muhammadan law*. 3rd ed. Bombay: n.p.

Usmani, Maulana Umar Ahmad. 1980. *Fiqh Al-Quran*. Karachi: n.p.

Zahra, Muhammad Abu. n.d. *Malik*. Cairo: Darul Fikhr Al-Arabi.

Zamakshari. 1977. *Al-Kashaf*. Beirut: Dar al-Ma'arif.

Zarakshi, Imam. 1980. *Al-Ijaba Li Irada Ma Istadrarathu Aisha Alal-Sahaba (Aisha's corrections of the statements of the companions)*. Beirut: Al-Maktab Al-Islam.

Index